T0128746

JAG

CHRISTIAN LESSONS FROM MY GOLDEN RETRIEVER

ANTHONY LOPEZ

ALSO INCLUDED IN THIS VOLUME

SEE YOU AT THE WAKE
2ND EDITION
HEALING RELATIONSHIPS
BEFORE IT'S TOO LATE

authorHOUSE®

AuthorHouse™
1663 Liberty Drive
Bloomington, IN 47403
www.authorhouse.com
Phone: 1-800-839-8640

First published by AuthorHouse 11/30/2011

ISBN: 978-1-4670-2695-6 (sc)
ISBN: 978-1-4670-2694-9 (hc)
ISBN: 978-1-4670-2693-2 (e)

Library of Congress Control Number: 2011916134
Bible scripture taken from the New International Version

Printed in the United States of America

Mom, I miss you

ACKNOWLEDGEMENTS

There are many people to whom I am grateful for helping me become the person that I am today. Above all, I am most sincerely grateful to my family. My better half and life-partner, Yvette, who has been by my side since we were both barely sixteen years old: I love you and thank you for all of your support and encouragement over the years. To my daughters Cristina and Marisa: I am so proud to be your father. You inspire me to constantly try to be a better human being because I want to be the best father that I can be for you. To my brother Louie: you are a great friend. Thank you. To the greatest Dad in the world, my father Hector Luis Lopez Sr.: you have been a wonderful father. You and Mom sacrificed everything so that Louie and I could have it all. From you I have learned much, especially the meaning of loyalty. I love you. Finally, Mom: you shaped my life in ways that I am only now beginning to understand. Thank you for all your sacrifices. I miss you very much and I look forward to our heavenly reunion one day. I am also grateful to my dear friends and teachers, Pastor D.E. Rabineau of Evangel Chapel in Somerville, New Jersey and Pastor Rick Hawks of The Chapel in Fort Wayne, Indiana. You are good, principled and Christian men. I thank you for your example and for your teachings. Special thanks to Pamela Suárez who wonderfully edited the book and made it much better than I could have hoped for. Finally, to my dog Jag: you have been a good friend and companion. You have brought great joy to our family and for that I will always be grateful.

I wrote these two short books first as a reminder to myself of the ways that I hope I will behave as I strive to live a Christian life. I am a work in progress and God is not done with me yet. It is my sincere hope that they will, albeit in a small way, touch the lives of others.

TABLE OF CONTENTS

Acknowledgements..vii

Section I
JAG
Christian Lessons from My Golden Retriever

Foreword...1
Introduction 3
Chapter One..5
    Love Unconditionally
Chapter Two..11
    Be Happy Often
Chapter Three 17
    Never Pass Up a Hug
Chapter Four..21
    Look for Opportunities to Share with the People You Love
Chapter Five 25
    Sometimes the Best Thing to Say Is Nothing at All
Chapter Six..29
    Protect Those You Love
Chapter Seven 35
    Be Happy When You See Loved Ones
Chapter Eight..39
    Trust but Verify
Chapter Nine 45
    Be Humble
Chapter Ten 49
    Respect and Obey Your Master

Chapter Eleven..53
   Allow Yourself to be Cared For
Chapter Twelve 57
   Play Often
Chapter Thirteen 61
   Don't Complain
Chapter Fourteen 65
   Don't Dwell on Yesterday and Don't Worry About Tomorrow
Chapter Fifteen...69
   Be Sorry When You Pee On the Rug
Chapter Sixteen 73
   Ask for Help When You are Afraid
Epilogue 77

Section II
See You at the Wake
Healing Relationships Before It's Too Late

Foreword..83
The Long Ride Home 85
Introduction 91
Chapter One..95
   Why Family Members Fight
Chapter Two...111
   Reasons and Excuses
Chapter Three 123
   Common Themes
Chapter Four..133
   What Keeps Us Apart?
Chapter Five 151
   Creating Reconciliation
Chapter Six..161
   Preparing for Reconciliation
Chapter Seven 173
   Keeping the Peace

SECTION I

JAG

CHRISTIAN LESSONS FROM MY GOLDEN RETRIEVER

ANTHONY B. LÓPEZ

FOREWORD

Life's cadence has a tendency to set its own pace. If you are anything like me, you may be finding that life almost never slows down. In fact, I believe that the older we get, the faster times flies by. That is why every once in a while we have to force ourselves to take a deep breath, take a hard look in the mirror, and answer a few questions: am I living the Christian life that God intended me to? Am I fulfilling His expectations and living up to my potential? When I stand before the Lord, will He say, "Well done, my good and faithful servant"? Oh, how we all long to hear those words!

Have you ever noticed that some of life's best lessons are learned serendipitously? It's not until after we've experienced something in our life that we look back and nod our head as if to say, "now I get it." Experience and The School of Hard Knocks are the best human institutions to teach us what works and what doesn't. There are times when those lessons can be quite costly and painful. Thank God, there are other ways for us to learn. We can learn from observing others and from modeling those living godly and good lives. We certainly can and must learn from the written word of God: the Bible. It is the most complete how-to guide on living a good life that has ever been written. When it comes to leading a Christian life, we can learn from all kinds of sources – including one of God's creations and man's best friend, a dog.

I've known Anthony "Tony" Lopez for nearly ten years. To say that he has a gift for making the complex seem simple is an understatement. He has a way of teaching us profound, God-centered principles with an abundance of common sense in an entertaining and practical way. In his book *JAG: Christian Lessons Learned from My Golden Retriever*, Tony captures some timeless lessons that when applied daily will enrich our lives and the lives of those around us. Read this book with an open heart and allow it to minister to you. If we each apply the Christian principles and lessons outlined in the book, I am certain we will make a greater impact in our world – and we will lead happier lives.

Rick Hawks
Senior Pastor
The Chapel
Fort Wayne, Indiana

INTRODUCTION

His name is Judge Advocate General. That is the name of my four-legged best friend. We call him Jag. Jag has been a part of our family for ten years. From the first day we brought him home as a tiny puppy, Jag has been a loyal friend and companion. He has given unselfishly of his love and affection. He has trusted more than he should. I don't think he has had a moment of worry and as far as I can tell he has never gone to bed angry. He has never refused to be hugged or to give a hug. Jag has protected our home in his own friendly way, threatening to lick to death any intruder that would even think about breaking in. Always at the ready to play, Jag has an uncanny ability to bring his blanket to encourage a game of tug-of-war at exactly the right times.

Jag has sat quietly at our feet when it was best not to say anything. Like a shadow he moves from one room to the next, always finding a spot near where we are sitting or standing, just in case he is needed – or in the event that an impromptu belly rub might break out. Jag has never complained when he is sick and just allows himself to be cared for. He always seeks refuge next to our bed when the thunder booms in the middle of the night. Jag is always sorry when he does something he's not supposed to, although that happens infrequently. He does not like to have a bath, but submits to them humbly and patiently, obeying every command to "stay." Jag is sad when we leave and always happy to see us when we come back.

Over the years that Jag has been with us, he has taught me more about how to be a good Christian than almost anyone else. He has modeled the behaviors that I want to emulate each and every day in my life. Imagine if we could all do what Jag does? It would be a much happier world for all of us.

Jag is eleven years old now. I don't like thinking about it much, but I realize that he probably will not be with us too many more years. But his impact on our lives will remain with us for as long as we live. I enjoy every moment that I spend with Jag and I learn from him every single day. The lessons captured here are timeless. I wish they were my own because they are brilliant, albeit simple. But they are not mine at all. I'm just the observer who wrote them down; Jag is the author and the teacher.

CHAPTER ONE

Love Unconditionally

John 15:12-14

My command is this: Love each other as I have loved you.
Greater love has no one than this, that he lay down his life
for his friends.

Anyone who has experienced the joy of having a dog has likely experienced the unconditional love that these creatures have the ability to give. From day one, even as a tiny puppy, Jag has showered our family with unconditional love. Before glancing over that last sentence and moving on casually, we should pause and really think about what it means. Unconditional love is easy to say, but much harder to practice. Love is the most powerful of emotions. It implies and represents so much that from the beginning of time it has defined one of the most important elements of the human psyche. An often overused word, love transcends many dimensions of our existence.

In the end, love is something we search for and long for. We cherish it when we have it, mourn when we lose it, and are sometimes cautious before we grant it. We talk about falling in and out of love, although that seems to be in stark contrast with the concept of unconditional love. We say we love this or that – even a food like pizza. But that's not love, that's *like*.

Try this for a moment: define the word *love*. It's not easy, is it? But can you recognize it when you see it or when you feel it? I bet you can.

We know love because instinctively we recognize that it implies a strong affection for another. It gives rise to our desire for the other person's well being and happiness, even more than our own – like the love a parent feels for a child. We know love because instinctively we have an attachment or devotion to someone, as in the love we feel for a sibling or our best friend. For the most blessed among us, we know love because we've felt the fatherly concern of God for humankind, and we adore and love God. However, we should never underestimate the power of love and what it really means. We ought not take it for granted or allow its casual use in our everyday vernacular to diminish its significance and impact on our lives.

The best definition of love is found in scripture.

<u>1 Corinthians 13: 4-7</u>

Love is patient, love is kind. It does not envy, it does not boast, it is not proud. It is not rude, it is not self-seeking, it is not easily angered, it keeps no record of wrongs. ⁶Love does not delight in evil but rejoices with the truth. ⁷It always protects, always trusts, always hopes, always perseveres.

Jag understands love. More importantly, he understands the principle of unconditional love!

I looked up the word "unconditional" in Webster's *New World Thesaurus* because I wanted to know what other words were associated with it. It seems obvious enough doesn't it? To most of us, "unconditional" means *without reservation* or *free of attachments*. But the word takes on its real meaning and strength when you consider the other words used to describe it. Words such as positive, definite, absolute, unconstrained, outright, final, certain, complete, entire, whole, unrestricted, unqualified, and unlimited are just a few of the words used to describe unconditional. Unconditional is also interchangeable with actual, thorough, genuine, indubitable, assured, determinate, unequivocal, categorical, decisive, unmistakable, clear, and unquestionable.

Can you think of a few things that qualify as unconditional? I mean *really* unconditional? It seems to me almost everything in life has some conditions attached to it. Whether spelled out in specific detailed contracts or agreements between people, or implied with a handshake, most every transaction in life has some conditions attached to it. There is almost always a catch. Otherwise, phrases such as "if it sounds too good to be true, it probably is" and "buyers beware" would have no meaning or place in society. What would attorneys do for a living if there was no need for setting or enforcing contracts with all sorts of conditions? Isn't that what the concept of *quid pro quo* is really all about?

Quid pro quo. It sounds so elegant when spoken. After all, it's Latin, and when said with a certain flair it makes the person using it sound intellectual and sophisticated. The very meaning of the phrase implies that there are conditions. It means "something for something." It indicates a more or less equal exchange or substitution of goods or services. Said another way – although not quite as elegantly – is *tit for tat.*

Despite the fact that *tit for tat* sounds more like what two toddlers might say to each other in the sand box – "you give me 'tit' and I'll give you 'tat', the concept basically means "you take care of me, and I'll take care of you." Nothing can be less unconditional than that!

Quid pro quo more aptly defines most of our relationships, both business and personal, than almost any other phrase. Certainly in business there is a clear *quid pro quo*. I do some work for you, and you pay me. *Quid pro quo.* I paid for breakfast this time; you pick it up the next. *Quid pro quo.* I say something nice about you and you say something nice back. *Quid pro quo.* I hurl an insult at you; you launch one right back at me. *Quid pro quo.* I bring you chicken soup when you're not feeling well and you walk my dog when I need to go out of town. *Quid pro quo.* That doesn't sound too bad, right? After all, what's wrong with expecting a bit in return for our good deeds? On the surface, it seems like a good system. So, that begs the question: why does it break down so often?

A short story may illustrate the primary reason that the *quid pro quo* system is so fragile:

A man moved to San Francisco to start a new job. He was new to the area, so it was taking him a bit of time to adjust to his new home and environment. One day, after he had been in his new job about two months, he was having lunch with a co-worker. The co-worker asked how he was enjoying living in San Francisco. The man said he liked it fine, but was finding the people a bit cold and unfriendly. This surprised the co-worker, who had a completely different impression of his hometown.

So he asked why the man felt that way. The man explained that each day he would go for a morning jog along the bay close to the Golden Gate Bridge. He noted that none of the other joggers ever said a word to him; they just ran past and never even said good morning. Again the co-worker was surprised. He too was a jogger and always found people to be very friendly when running past him. So he invited the man to join him to jog together. The man agreed and they both met the next morning and went for a run. At the end of their run, the co-worker turned to the man and said, "See? Everyone was very friendly and everyone said good morning." The man looked at his co-worker and said, "Yes, but you always said it first."

Therein lies the primary reason why *quid pro quo* is an unsustainable system. Someone has to be willing to go first. By going first we take a risk that the good deed, or the investment we are making, will not be reciprocated. Then what do we do? Do we try again? If so, how many times? I mean, if you buy lunch for a friend and next time he does not offer to return the favor, how many times will you buy him lunch if he never even offers to pick up the tab from time to time? *Quid pro quo* breaks down quickly if one party feels like the relationship is one sided, and the benefit consistently favors one over the other. Divorce attorneys make their living from marriages that try to survive exclusively on *quid pro quo*. Let's face it, how many of us really mean it when we say "for better or for worse; in sickness or in health, until death do us part?" Statistically speaking the answer is less than 50% of us.

Human nature makes it is nearly impossible for us to experience or impart unconditional anything. Our sense of fair play, which is woven into the fabric of our DNA, makes it difficult for us to do something for someone totally unconditionally. It may be polite to say "don't mention it" when someone thanks us for doing something for them; but God forbid they forget to say thank you in the first place! It may leave us feeling a bit taken advantage of, and for most of us, it would make us think twice before offering to help again.

If giving unconditionally is so hard – whether it's our money, our time or even a compliment – how could we then expect that we are capable of giving unconditional *love*? It's tough, but not impossible. We can all think of some great examples of people who have modeled unconditional love. Maybe one of the best examples is the one Mother Teresa gave us.

She dedicated her entire life to caring for others in the most difficult of circumstances.

Nearly sixty years ago Mother Teresa founded the Missionaries of Charity in Calcutta, India. She spent more than 45 years ministering to the poor, sick, orphaned and dying. I had a chance to go on a short mission's trip to Haiti in July 2009. I was only there for one week. I saw people living in conditions that broke my heart. I saw people of all ages who seemed without hope; dirty, hungry, homeless, forgotten people. Our team ministered to them and loved them as much as we could in the short period of time we were there. Mother Teresa did that for 45 years! Her kindness and unconditional love inspired an entire movement and have given us all a beautiful role model to follow.

Yet no one has demonstrated unconditional love better than God our Father.

<u>John 3:16</u>

For God so loved the world that He gave His one and only Son, that whoever believes in Him shall not perish but have eternal life.

That's unconditional love!

We should all strive to love unconditionally. When in doubt, follow the example set by my good friend Jag. He seems to understand that unconditional love is the kind of love that takes on the characteristics found in scripture.

CHAPTER TWO

Be Happy Often

Jag likes to sleep lying on the cool marble tile floor of the foyer in our home. As an early riser, I am usually up and about the house before everyone else. It is always fun for me to hear the thump thump thump of Jag's tail slapping on the floor even before I turn the corner as I make my way to the foyer where I know he will be. Even before he sees me, he hears me coming, and his tail begins to dance. He does not move another muscle as he anticipates my arrival, but his eyes are looking directly at the spot he knows I will be in just a moment, and his tail says, "Good morning, Dad!" It sometimes makes me wish my daughters had tails!

Have you ever wondered why dogs wag their tails? Well, I have. Dr. Stanley Coren wrote this in his book entitled *How to Speak Dog*:

> *....In some ways, tail-wagging serves the same functions as our human smile, polite greeting, or nod of recognition. Smiles are social signals, and human beings seem to reserve most of their smiles for social situations, where somebody is around to see them. Sometimes, vicarious social situations, as when watching television or occasionally when thinking about somebody special, can trigger a smile. For dogs, the tail wag seems to have the same properties. A dog will wag its tail for a person or another dog. It may wag its tail for a cat, horse, mouse, or perhaps even a butterfly. But when the dog is by itself, it will not wag its tail to any lifeless thing. If you put a bowl of food down, the dog will wag its tail to*

11

> *express its gratitude to you. In contrast, when the dog walks into a room and finds its bowl full, it will approach and eat the food just as happily, but with no tail-wagging other than perhaps a slight excitement tremor. This is one indication that tail-wagging is meant as communication or language. In the same way that we don't talk to walls, dogs don't wag their tails to things that are not apparently alive and socially responsive.*

> *A dog's tail speaks volumes about his mental state, his social position, and his intentions. How the tail came to be a communication device is an interesting story. The dog's tail was originally designed to assist the dog in its balance.... However evolution again seized an opportunity and now adapted the tail for communication purposes.*

It seems to me we all need to wag our tails more often! We all need to strive to be happy more often. It is a choice we get to make every hour of every day. In most circumstances, we can choose to be happy. Life has a way of happening around us, and whether we like it or not there will be unhappy circumstances that will be a part of our lives. Losing a parent to cancer, as I did when my mother died at age sixty-four is an occasion to be unhappy. Watching your child go through a serious illness and being at the mercy of God and doctors to help her is a good excuse to be unhappy, too.

When a person you love betrays your confidence, that's a good reason to be unhappy. If your house burns down and everything you own is gone, it may be reasonable to be unhappy. There might be other reasons. But by and large, the things we allow to make us unhappy are silly. For instance, being unhappy because your favorite team lost the big football game over the weekend is silly. Being unhappy because your daughter dinged up the car as she was pulling out of the garage is silly, too. (Don't ask me how I know this.) In the end, what we choose to be happy or unhappy about is entirely up to us. How often we decide to be unhappy and how long we choose to stay that way is also up to us.

We've all heard the old adage that "it takes more muscles to frown than to smile, so smile more often." I found a raging debate online with many articles on the subject of whether it takes more effort to smile or to frown. Some claim it takes 43 muscles to frown and 17 to smile, others say it takes 26 to smile and 62 to frown. Naysayers claim it's quite the opposite, that in fact it takes more muscles to smile than to frown. Some studies have been done to determine if we burn more calories when we smile or frown! Amazing. Does it really matter? What if we just apply a healthy dose of common sense to this debate? The bottom line is this: smile and people smile back. Frown and guess what? People frown back at you. You choose.

When we make facial expressions, we're essentially transmitting volumes of information that can be received, read and interpreted by others. When we smile we transmit a signal of friendliness that transcends cultural barriers. Smile at someone in Brazil and you will likely get a similar reaction as if you smile at someone in South Africa. Try the same with a frown, and lo and behold, the same thing happens! So we can try to analyze the 43 muscles in the face, most of which are controlled by the seventh cranial nerve that exists in the cerebral cortex and emerges from your skull just in front of your ears before it splits into five primary branches: temporal, zygomatic, buccal, mandibular and cervical. Or we can exercise them and smile. Again, the choice is yours and yours alone.

Interestingly, humans don't have a monopoly on facial expressions. Many primates, especially apes, have many of the same expressive muscles that we do and use them to convey similar emotional information. I am convinced that Jag smiles at me. I have no problem knowing when he is happy. His tail and his body language make that clear to me; and he is happy often.

If an apple a day keeps the dentist away, then laughing out loud each day will keep your cardiologist away. There is some evidence to suggest that laughing each day may help prevent a heart attack. Who would have thought that laughter, along with an active sense of humor, may help protect you from heart disease? Humor is infectious. The sound of roaring laughter is far more contagious than any cough, sniffle, or sneeze. When laughter is shared, it binds people together and increases happiness and intimacy. Moreover, laughter triggers healthy physical changes in the body. Humor and laughter strengthen your immune system, boost your energy, diminish pain, and protect you from the damaging effects of stress. Oh, and by the way, it's free.

I have never experienced a better example of the power of happiness and laughter than during my mission trip to Haiti. It was incredibly hot as I mounted the school bus in the middle of the afternoon. We were getting ready to make our way to a few remote villages to minister to the people there. The bus was filled with our mission team members and local Haitians, most of whom worked at the Missions Of Hope. We were making our way down a bumpy, dusty mountain road when the bus' engine stopped. Despite our driver's best efforts, the bus would not start up again. Even with the windows open, no breeze was coming through the bus, so the temperature quickly started to climb and it became quite uncomfortable.

I remember how I felt immediately after the bus broke down. I was not a happy camper. I was hot, thirsty and tired. Thank God I did not start to complain out loud, but in my mind I was whining like a school boy. Suddenly one of the Haitian locals piped up and said, "Let's sing Christian songs!" He said it enthusiastically and with passion. I thought to myself, *Is he serious? Sing? Now? Wouldn't it be more productive to get out of the bus and push?*

It did not take more than a few seconds after the young man suggested that we start singing Christian songs that he had almost everyone else in the bus agreeing with him. People broke out in song and the bus was filled with the beautiful sound of Christian contemporary music. We were having church in that bus! Even I got wrapped up in the singing. We clapped our hands, used the back of the seats as drums, and even stomped our feet to keep the beat of the music. The bus felt like it was jumping off the rocky road. This went on for twenty minutes or more. It was wonderful.

Finally another bus arrived and we were able to get back on the road and onto the agenda for the rest of the afternoon. As I sat quietly looking out the window, I saw abject poverty all around me. The homes were made of little more than tin planks, cardboard and in some cases, cement blocks. Most of the homes had dirt floors, no running water, and only grimy sheets for windows. It occurred to me that this was the home of the people who just a short while ago had been singing loud and joyful praises to God in a sweltering broken down bus. I felt ashamed. My first thought was to complain; their first thought was to be happy and make the best of it. They may be financially poor, but they are rich in spirit and they have happiness in their souls. That day, inside a hot and dusty bus, I learned the true value and meaning of being happy.

Being happy and laughing often is a powerful antidote to stress. No pills work faster and more reliably to bring your mind into focus and balance than a hardy laugh. Doctors agree that a good laugh lightens our burdens, raises our level of hope, and helps our minds stay alert. Experts say that laughter boosts our immune system, triggers the release of endorphins (the body's natural feel-good chemical), and protects our heart. Doctors at Maryland's Medical Center in Boston did a study and found that people with heart disease were 40% less likely to laugh in a variety of situations compared to people of the same age without heart disease. In the study, researchers compared the humor responses of 300 people. Half of the participants had either suffered a heart attack or undergone coronary bypass surgery. The other 150 did not have heart disease.

The most significant finding was that people with heart disease responded less humorously to everyday life situations. They generally laughed less, even in positive situations, and they displayed more anger and hostility. Bah humbug! It seems the grouches lose again. Learn from Jag, who will not die of a heart attack: Lighten up, smile, laugh, and be happy more often. If you've got to die of something, die because you lost your breath laughing too hard.

Go ahead, wag your tail!

CHAPTER THREE

Never Pass Up a Hug

<u>Genesis 29:12-14</u>

As soon as Laban heard the news about Jacob, his sister's son, he hurried to meet him. He embraced him and kissed him and brought him to his home, and there Jacob told him all these things. Then Laban said to him, "You are my own flesh and blood."

When I am at home, Jag is never too far away. Often, I am not even aware that he is sitting or lying nearby. Sometimes I think that a better name for him would have been Shadow because that's just what he is like. He's just there. Like a shadow, you are not always aware that it's there, but it is. I noticed something else about this quality of Jag's: I find it endearing. It makes me feel so good to know that he wants nothing more than to be close to me.

If I go to the gym downstairs to work out, he quietly makes his way down the stairs and finds a spot just outside the door of the room and waits patiently. If I step out into the garage to do some work on the car or to do a bit of cleaning, he follows me out, finds a place to lie down and patiently waits for me to be done. When I go to my office to do some writing, he is never more than fifteen feet away. I move, he moves. He's my shadow. So why does Jag do that? I think the answer is simple: he often gets a hug. If I get up and walk past him, he gets a hug. As I move from one room to the next, I often pause and pet him, hug him, and tell him he's a good boy. Thump thump thump goes his tail and I can see him smile at me. Jag never passes up a chance to get a hug. And here's the best part – I never feel better than when I am giving him one!

Hugs feel good to both the giver and the receiver. As you would expect there are great medical reasons why giving and receiving hugs is a good thing, and it turns out their effects are more than skin deep. A study by University of North Carolina researchers found that hugs increase the "bonding" hormone oxytocin and decrease the risk of heart disease. The study found that when couples hugged for twenty seconds, their levels of oxytocin, which are also released during childbirth and breastfeeding, increased. The study also found that people in loving relationships had the highest increases. Additionally, levels of the stress hormone cortisol decreased in women, as did their blood pressure.

The positive effects of hugs are not just chemical, but they are physical and emotional as well. A hug communicates many things to people. It can bring back fond memories and helps people recall joyful times spent together. Think of the joy of hugging a family member when you meet them at the airport after not having seen them in a long time. Does anything feel better than that? Our heart races with anticipation and joy as we anxiously await their arrival, and even run into each other's arms when we finally see the person. Hugs are uniquely able to connect us to other human beings in a way that is hard to find in our modern world. You can't hug a text message. And while an email Hallmark card may be cute, it's not warm and tight like a good hug should be.

Perhaps no story illustrates the power of a hug better than the tale of Esau and Jacob. In the book of Genesis we learn the story of these two estranged brothers who spent years apart because of a feud they'd had as young men. Jacob robbed Esau of his father's blessing, which was his birthright. For years Esau's anger boiled over for Jacob and he even threatened to kill him. Esau escaped and left to build his life someplace else. But as in most of our lives, there comes a time when we realize that material wealth does not bring happiness. We realize that the love of family and friends is far more important than anything else we can possess. So Esau decides to go home to meet with his brother and beg for his forgiveness. From the story in Genesis we see that Jacob was anxious and afraid of how his brother might react:

<u>Genesis 33:1-3</u>

Jacob looked up and there was Esau, coming with his four hundred men; so he divided the children among Leah, Rachel and the two maidservants. He put the maidservants and their children in front, Leah and her children next, and Rachel and Joseph in the rear. He himself went on ahead and bowed down to the ground seven times as he approached his brother.

And here's how Esau reacted:

<u>Genesis 33:4</u>

But Esau ran to meet Jacob and embraced him; he threw his arms around his neck and kissed him. And they wept.

Just as they did in ancient times, hugs can have a healing effect on today's broken relationship. They are a sign of peace and love. In our modern world, we seem to be trying hard to replace the all-natural, original hug with virtual fakes. One of my favorite ways to end an email message to someone I am close to is by writing *un fuerte abrazo,* which is Spanish for "a strong hug." It's the best I can do in an email since I can't actually hug the person. I reserve that closing statement in my emails for the people I care about the most; my close friends and family – my loved ones.

The benefits of hugs cannot be overstated. Humans are clearly social animals. We crave social interaction and the touch of another human being. There is clear evidence that babies who are not hugged and nurtured from an early age often grow up to be detached adults who struggle with intimacy and have difficulty creating loving relationships. The therapeutic touch of one person to another has been shown to reduce stress and pain among adults. It has even been linked to possibly reducing the symptoms of Alzheimer's disease. We need hugs. And like Jag, we need to find ways of creating opportunities for hugs to take place.

Here are a few simple Rules for Hugging straight from my best buddy Jag, who is an expert on the subject:

- Always stop what you are doing for a hug.
- Be ready to give a hug.
- Be ready to receive a hug.
- Be accessible without being in the way. You never know when a hug opportunity will arise.

CHAPTER FOUR

Look for Opportunities to Share with the People You Love

Luke 10: 41-42

"Martha, Martha," the Lord answered, "you are worried and upset about many things, but only one thing is needed. Mary has chosen what is better, and it will not be taken away from her."

Jag is never far away from us. Like a faithful and loyal companion, he seems to always be close. I think he does it because he does not want to miss out on any of the family action. When a few of us are sitting in the family room together, Jag makes his way nearby, makes his presence known - just in case anyone missed him - and lies down with a loud sigh as if he's had a very tough day. Each time he does it, it makes us chuckle. He's just that cute.

If we move into the bedroom to watch television or to have a chat, he slips into the room, sits quietly at doorway and waits. If he hears laughter, he assumes he's missing a party and with tail wagging, he joins in. If he senses that there's a need for a party to start, he is not afraid to grab his blanket and challenge one of us to a fun game of tug of war. Jag is an opportunist. He knows that if he's just available and grabs one of us with his big brown puppy eyes, something good is going to happen.

I'm reminded of a story about a little boy who, on a beautiful autumn morning, accompanies his mother to visit her father's grave. As she gently sweeps some fallen leaves off the top of the grave with her gloved hand, the little boy reads the tombstone.

"Mommy, why does it say May 3, 1925 dash August 24, 2006?" he asks.

She smiles at him and answers tenderly, "That means that Grandpa was born on May 3, 1925 and he died on August 24, 2006."

The little boy thinks about that for a moment. Then, with pure innocence in his voice, he says, "So that means that the dash was Grandpa's life."

Life is short. Sometimes it's as short as a dash on a tombstone. Those of us who have older children understand that all too well. Our kids are born and then we blink and they are all grown up. Not long ago, wiser older folks would caution me to enjoy my kids while they were still small because they grow up so fast. I'd always smile and say, "I will." Suddenly I'm the one advising the young parents to enjoy their kids while they are young. And they always smile and say, "We will."

But all too often, we don't. Life gets in the way. There are planes to catch, customers to visit and careers to build. There is money that has to be made, houses and cars that need to be purchased and college tuition to saved for. And just when we think we are almost done, we get the urge to own that lake house. We reason that if we can just have the lake house, we'll have a place to spend more time with the family. Of course, what's a lake house if you don't have the boat and the jet skis to go with it? So, just a few more hours of overtime, a few more business trips, and a few more late night dinner meetings and you'll be done. It's a mouse trap! They don't call it the rat race for nothing.

I am as experienced as any other mouse in the rat race. In fact, I'd say I was winning the rat race for a while. I was at the head of the rat pack, with all the other rats chasing me. Evidence of my success was easy to see: We had a nice house on the 13th green of a golf course, a few nice cars in the garage and a bit of money in the bank. We enjoyed a vacation or two, and we have tons of pictures and videos of Christmas mornings with dozens of gifts under the tree. Business was booming. I was traveling the world playing Mr. Jet Setter. I had Executive Platinum status on American Airlines and Platinum status on Continental Airlines – both in the same year! I was forced to get a new passport because I used up all the pages in the old one.

Then one day I blinked. Yvette and I have been married twenty five years. Cristina is twenty one years old, and Marisa is sixteen going on twenty-one. Jag is nearly twelve years old, and Golden Retrievers don't usually live much past fourteen. I thank God that I have been able to spend as much time with my family as I have. And I kick myself in the rear for allowing so many precious hours and so much of my energy to go to less important things. The good news is that I'm learning a thing or two from Jag, and I will keep trying to create even more opportunities to share with those I love.

In 1974 Harry Chapin released his song *Cat's in the Cradle*. It was from his album *Verities & Balderdash*. The single topped the charts in December 1974 and was Chapin's only number one song. It has become his best known work and a song that has transcended generations. The lyrics to the song were written by Chapin's wife, Sandy. They tell a story that sadly repeats itself over and over again in families all around the world: the story of a father who is so busy trying to make a living that he fails to make a life.

This father has a son who craves his attention and who repeatedly asks his daddy to play with him. But the dad always responds with a promise that they will spend time together "later." The boy, who admires and loves his daddy, says he wants to be just like him when he grows up. As in real life, the boy grows up all too quickly. The song's third verse tells of a son now having his own life in college and the father wanting to spend time with him. However, the son does not have time for his father, as he is pursuing his own life.

As the years pass the man retires from work and is free to spend time anyway he pleases. His greatest desire is to spend time with his son, who by now has a family of his own. His son has all the stresses of life on him and while he responds warmly to his father's request to spend some time with him, he tells him that he just doesn't have the time right now, and promises that they'll get together in the future. And the cycle of life seems complete. The boy had grown up to be just like his dad. A good man trapped in the pursuit of the pointless and missing the point. God forbid this happens to us.

The irony illustrated in the song is accentuated by the use of the nursery rhymes Cat's Cradle, Silver Spoon, Little Boy Blue, and Man in the Moon in the chorus. No man has ever regretted spending too much time with his children growing up. I've simply never heard anyone ever say, "I wasted too much time with my kids when they were young. I should have worked more." Sadly, the contrary of that statement is much more common.

In Luke 10:38-42, Jesus reminds Martha and all of us to focus on what's important. While Jesus was visiting Martha and her sister Mary, Martha busied herself serving her guest. No doubt she was trying desperately to be a great hostess. Her sister sat at Jesus' feet and listened to Him.

Luke 10:38-42

38As Jesus and His disciples were on their way, He came to a village where a woman named Martha opened her home to Him. 39She had a sister called Mary, who sat at the Lord's feet listening to what He said. 40But Martha was distracted by all the preparations that had to be made. She came to Him and asked, "Lord, don't you care that my sister has left me to do the work by myself? Tell her to help me!"

41"Martha, Martha," the Lord answered, "you are worried and upset about many things, 42but only one thing is needed. Mary has chosen what is better, and it will not be taken away from her."

When Martha complained to the Lord and tattled on her sister, Jesus gently but firmly corrected her. In today's vernacular, Jesus was telling her to take a chill pill, enjoy the moment and don't worry about the trivial things. Jesus Christ was in her living room! What could be more important? And what better reason to spend time with someone you love? We all need to be more like Mary and choose wisely how we spend our time. Be an opportunist like Jag and create more moments to spend with those we love. Remember, life is only a dash.

CHAPTER FIVE

Sometimes the Best Thing to Say Is Nothing at All

I am not sure how he does it, but it seems to me that Jag knows when I need him to simply sit next to me and just be quiet. Perhaps it has been a long, hard day and I would rather not talk about it with anyone. Maybe we've just received bad news about something unexpected and more than anything else we just want to sit quietly and think. Everyone has days like that, and when we have those days it is good to know that we have someone to be supportive and available. However, well-intentioned people often want to talk through the issue. In an attempt to show someone we care and want to help, we try to find just the right words to say. Not so with Jag. He somehow senses the mood and knows that sometimes, the best thing is to simply be available and quiet. No tug of war games and no insisting on a belly rub.

When my mother died in December 2003, I went into what I can only describe as problem-solving mode. I guess it was my way of coping. I took care of the arrangements with the funeral home, made the necessary announcements to our family and friends, and made arrangements for my wife and daughters to fly home to New Jersey from Indiana where we lived at the time. I suppose that staying busy was my way of avoiding the grief of losing my mom. The morning that I arrived at the funeral home for the wake, I was the first person in my family to see my mother. She looked beautiful. She was a beautiful woman. A short while later, other family and friends began to arrive.

I was very happy to see my good friend Kiko Morillo when he arrived at the funeral home. I knew that with him I would have refuge; that he would provide some normalcy and stability in the midst of what was about to become an unsettling grieving experience for my family. The hardest part came when my wife and two daughters arrived. Both of my daughters had been very close with Grandma. Marisa was only nine years old. Cristina was fourteen. When I saw them at the door, I immediately went to meet them. I knelt before Marisa and asked if she was okay with seeing Grandma and she said she was. So I held hands with both of my daughters and we walked up to the casket. Soon, they were both crying and my heart was breaking. For the first time since my mother had died, I was crying, too – not only because my mom was dead, but also because it was so hard to see my daughters and wife experiencing such pain and grief.

It took some minutes, but I finally managed to calm the girls down a bit. I remember kneeling in front of Marisa and holding her for a long while as she cried on my shoulder. I kept telling her it was going to be okay, but she could not see the tears running down my face. Finally Marisa stopped crying and I was able to let her go. Dejected, I quietly walked over to my friend Kiko with my head held low. I stood next to him, staring at the floor with my arms folded. After awhile, Kiko said the only thing that would have made any sense at that moment.

"Well, that pretty much sucked," he declared.

"Yep," I replied, looking at him with tears in my eyes. I returned my gaze to the floor, and we stood together in silence for the longest time. Words were not necessary. I knew my friend was suffering with me –that he was there for me. And that's exactly what I needed at that moment. Others might have been tempted to console me by assuring me that everything would be okay, and that time heals all. There is nothing wrong with trying to be supportive and consoling people who are in pain. But often, a calm and silent presence says more than any eloquent words ever could.

There is no verifiable scientific proof that dogs can pick up on human emotions. Yet they seem to have an uncanny ability to know just how to behave and how to react depending on the mood and needs of their master. From an evolutionary point of view, it would be very strange if dogs did not have the ability to sense mood and that the human animal was the first to develop that skill. I know this: my friend Jag senses my emotional state of mind just fine. When I'm happy, he's happy. When I am sad, he seems sensitive to my mood. When I get angry, he knows it.

And on the days when things pretty much suck, he's always there for me – a calm and silent presence.

CHAPTER SIX

Protect Those You Love

Few things are more startling than having the phone ring in the middle of the night. It abruptly slams you back to reality from a deep sleep and you literally jump in your bed. The same thing happens to us when Jag lets out a few loud barks in the wee hours of the morning. If he's heard something unusual he announces it to the entire household. He does the same thing when the sump pump alarm sounds in the basement. The alarm is designed to go off if the pump fails, but it's difficult for us to hear when we are upstairs, especially if we are in our bedroom. So Jag serves as our own living, breathing backup alarm system, barking to let us know something is not right.

When we are playing with Jag and he barks, we can tell it's his "playing voice." But his bark is totally different when there's trouble in the house. When he is serious and something is not right, his bark takes on a grave tone. The reality is that Jag is a gentle giant. We don't know how he would act if he really needed to protect us against an intruder or some other real danger. Happily we've never had to put that to the test. I suspect though, that if the time came for him to jump to action and actually protect us, he would do it even at the cost of his own life.

We have all heard stories of people doing incredible, even seemingly supernatural things when they are stressed. We've read reports of a parent lifting a car off their child who had been hit by the vehicle. Often it is the rush of adrenaline that our body produces in instances of high stress or physically exhilarating situations that gives us the boost of energy we need to do these Superman-like feats. Adrenaline is a hormone produced by the adrenal gland in the body of many animals. When it is produced in the body it stimulates the heart rate, dilates blood vessels and air passages, and has a number of other minor effects. But overall, it heightens our awareness and leads to the "fight or flight" response – the early evolutionary adaptation that helps us cope with dangerous and unexpected situations. I'm sure that a rush of adrenaline is in part what is driving Jag's behavior when he senses the need to protect his family and his home.

Whatever the source of our strength and courage, our instinct is to protect those we love. Every parent understands what this means. We would lay down our lives to protect our families, especially our children! Fortunately, most of us are not called to make that ultimate sacrifice. For most of us, protecting our family and loved ones is much less dramatic than this. We protect our family by taking care of their basic needs for food, shelter, medical care and other essentials. We protect our families by buying insurance if we can afford it to help minimize financial burdens in the event of a catastrophe. We protect our homes and families by installing an alarm system to discourage intruders. We even install smoke alarms to alert those we love in the event of a fire. We install carbon monoxide detectors to protect our families from a gas we can't even see or smell! Just as Jag instinctively protects those he loves, we all go to great lengths to protect our loved ones, too.

There is one more important way that we must protect those we love. We must protect them from falling victims to the trappings of the world. We must prepare our children to live *in* the world, but not to be *of* the world. We must help them to live a Christian life, protecting their souls and creating a loving environment where their relationships with Jesus Christ can flourish. I can think of no more important job as a father than protecting my daughters in this way – just as God the Father protects all of His children.

The Bible provides us with a great deal of evidence about how God protects and watches over us.

God protects us on our life journeys, as He did for the Hebrews when He freed them from bondage in Egypt:

<u>Joshua 24:16-18</u>

16 Then the people answered, "Far be it from us to forsake the LORD to serve other gods! [17] It was the LORD our God himself who brought us and our fathers up out of Egypt, from that land of slavery, and performed those great signs before our eyes. He protected us on our entire journey and among all the nations through which we traveled. [18] And the LORD drove out before us all the nations, including the Amorites, who lived in the land. We too will serve the LORD, because He is our God."

God protects us in times of trouble:

<u>Psalm 41:1-3</u>

[1] Blessed is he who has regard for the weak; the LORD delivers him in times of trouble. [2] The LORD will protect him and preserve his life; He will bless him in the land and not surrender him to the desire of his foes. [3] The LORD will sustain him on his sickbed and restore him from his bed of illness.

God protects us from evil's grip:

<u>2 Thessalonians 3:2-3</u>

[2] And pray that we may be delivered from wicked and evil men, for not everyone has faith. [3] But the Lord is faithful and He will strengthen and protect you from the evil one.

God protects and watches over us through our life's journey:

<u>Genesis 28:14-15</u>

[14] Your descendants will be like the dust of the earth, and you will spread out to the west and to the east, to the north and to the south. All peoples on earth will be blessed through you and your offspring. [15] I am with you and will watch over you wherever you go, and I will bring you back to this land. I will not leave you until I have done what I have promised you."

Psalm 121:6-8

⁶The sun will not harm you by day, nor the moon by night.
⁷ The LORD will keep you from all harm - He will watch
over your life; ⁸ the LORD will watch over your coming and
going both now and forevermore.

Finally, God will protect and watch over us, taking care to provide for our every physical, emotional, and psychological need. No passage in the Bible expresses that better than my favorite Psalm.

Psalm 23

¹The LORD is my shepherd, I shall not be in want.² He
makes me lie down in green pastures, He leads me beside
quiet waters, ³ He restores my soul. He guides me in paths
of righteousness for His name's sake.

⁴Even though I walk through the valley of the shadow of
death, I will fear no evil, for you are with me; your rod and
your staff, they comfort me.

⁵ You prepare a table before me in the presence of my enemies.
You anoint my head with oil; my cup overflows.

⁶ Surely goodness and love will follow me all the days of my
life, and I will dwell in the house of the LORD forever.

Psalm 23 is a wonderful statement of God's love and protection over us. The analogy of God as our shepherd with us as His sheep is beautiful. Sheep are simple animals. They also seem quite helpless. They need a shepherd that tends carefully to them and watches over them to keep them safe. More than this, they need a shepherd that goes above and beyond to save his sheep:

Matthew 18:12-14

¹²What do you think? If a man owns a hundred sheep, and

one of them wanders away, will he not leave the ninety-nine on the hills and go to look for the one that wandered off? ¹³And if he finds it, I tell you the truth, he is happier about that one sheep than about the ninety-nine that did not wander off. ¹⁴In the same way your Father in heaven is not willing that any of these little ones should be lost.

God is like that shepherd to each of us, protecting and saving us. In fact, He demonstrated the ultimate sign of His love and protection for us when He sacrificed His only Son Jesus so that we could be saved.

<u>John 3:16</u>

¹⁶For God so loved the world that He gave His one and only Son, that whoever believes in Him shall not perish but have eternal life.

Amen!

CHAPTER SEVEN

Be Happy When You See Loved Ones

Not long ago when my daughters were younger, I could always count on one thing when I got home from work: they would come running into my arms, all the way squealing with joy as they sang out, "Daaaaaaaaaaaaady's home!" And I would pick them up high in the air, give them a big hug and a kiss, and ask them, "So what did you do today?" Those were the good old days. What happened, you ask? They became teenagers.

My good friend and mentor Jesse Penn best described for me what I could expect from my daughters once they entered The Teenage Zone. The Teenage Zone is the place your kids go when they turn twelve or thirteen. It's dark and can be scary – for you, not for them. It's a place that you may or may not be invited to from time to time, although rest assured they are talking about you with the other kids who are in The Teenage Zone with them.

One afternoon, I called Jesse because I basically needed a friendly ear to do some venting – a kind way of saying I needed to whine a bit. He asked me how Cristina was. I huffed and started to tell him all about the latest "discussion" I was having with her. Cristina was not doing quite as well in school as I thought she could be doing. I recall being somewhat frustrated with my then 16-year old daughter. As I told Jesse the story, he began to laugh.

"What's so funny, Jesse?" I asked.

"Tony, right about now Cristina thinks you are about the biggest buffoon on the planet," Jesse replied with a chuckle. "She'll probably think that until she's about twenty-two or twenty-three years old. Then she'll start to realize that hey, maybe Dad wasn't that dumb after all, and she'll come back to you. But right now she's in The Zone."

Cristina is now twenty-one years old and I see the light at the end of the tunnel. Jesse was right – we may be out of The Teenage Zone in the very near future! Soon, I think Cristina may come to realize that over the last five years or so, her old Dad has miraculously gotten much smarter.

Well, I can always hope!

Jesse went on to tell me a short story about his mother.

"Tony," he began with a fatherly tone, "my mother went from thinking *summa cum laude* to just 'thank you Lordy.' She went from thinking her kids were going to be graduates of the top schools with top honors, to just being grateful we graduated high school!"

Now it was my turn to laugh. I could just see Mrs. Penn, a stern African American woman, saying exactly those words with a Southern Baptist gospel preaching tone in her voice. I understood Jesse's point immediately.

"So you're saying I need to take a deep breath and just be glad she's still in school, huh?"

"That's exactly what I'm saying," he answered. "Stay focused on the long term, and try not to worry too much about the everyday things that you really are not going to be able to control."

The times sure have changed. The little girls who once ran joyfully into my arms every time they saw me had left the world as we know it and entered into The Teenage Zone. I am sure they still love me. And all humor aside, my two daughters are both loving and caring young women who are not afraid to demonstrate emotion and love. But these days I can come home from work – or even from a long business trip – and it's entirely possible that I may be home for quite some time before they realize I have arrived. The good news is that once in a while they do have to come out of their rooms to get some food in the kitchen, and that's usually when they say, "Oh, hi Dad! When did you get home?" Having teenagers will humble you! As a daddy you must be prepared to go from being the center of your little girl's or little boy's universe to maybe having the same status that Pluto has in our solar system.

Thank God for Jag! Jag is always happy to see me. When I come home from any place, he's the first one at the door to greet me. I remember as a child watching the Flintstones cartoons. Every time Fred would come home, his faithful dog Dino would run to the door and tackle him to the ground, barking happily and licking his face just to say, "Hi, Master! Where have you been? I missed you!" Jag is just like Dino except he doesn't tackle me to the ground. Instead he does his own unique dance and whimpers with happiness. He runs around me and begs me to give him a hug and a good petting. Then he usually runs off, grabs his comfort blanket and brings it to me. He does the same thing to Mom and the girls, too. As soon as he hears the garage door opening, his ears perk up and he runs to the kitchen door that leads to the garage in anticipation that someone he loves is about to come through the door. I never get tired of Jag's welcome home ritual. I've learned from Jag that it's not enough to just be happy when we see someone we love. We also need to wag our tails and show it!

CHAPTER EIGHT

Trust but Verify

"Trust but verify" was one of Ronald Reagan's signature phrases. When he used this phrase, he was usually referring to relations with the Soviet Union. There is a uniquely special quality about that philosophy that appeals to me. It could be the New Yorker in me coming out, but it makes sense to me that checking something out even before trusting it is a good idea.

Jag is not a suspicious dog. In fact, he's probably too trusting. Whenever Jag encounters a stranger, whether human or canine, he's friendly. He's not afraid to get close and sniff his new found friend so as to check them out. Most of the time, he gives them his seal of approval. Interestingly though, he always looks to me for the okay before he gets too cozy with the stranger. He verifies his trust by getting my approval. Depending on how I am reacting toward them, he picks up on those signals and decides if he should continue getting closer to the stranger or if he should back off.

I see this behavior in Jag often, especially when I'm in the front yard of our home tending to the weeds – something I look forward to as much as I do my visits to the dentist. Jag is always out there with me, supervising my work while he watches the world go past. Invariably he will spot people who are walking across the street on the sidewalk, and he will sit up and follow them intently with his eyes. This is especially true if they have their dog walking along with them. Jag's tail will begin to wag and he gets a bit restless, but he will not move. He looks at them, then he looks at me, then he looks at them again. I can tell he wants desperately to run to them to say hello. But he waits for my approval. On the occasions when I recognize the folks walking along the sidewalk, I will wave and say hello. That's Jag's first indication that a party might be breaking out soon, so he waits for my signal. He looks at them, he looks at me, and he looks at them again. If I make my way over to the neighbors to start the conversation, Jag is in! He playfully bounds over to the folks and to his canine friend, and they do what they do best – sniff each other. However, if I keep weeding, he knows it's not okay to make his move. Jag trusts, but he verifies.

Certainly we would not want journalists to publish news reports without verifying their sources or checking their facts. We would not want to have a surgeon operate on us before we verified their diagnosis. It's not that we don't trust the doctor, but getting a second opinion is usually a good idea. We don't buy stock in a company or invest in a business until we've done our homework and checked out their business plan, balance sheets, and other important financial indicators. If we did, it would be called gambling rather than investing. "Trust but verify" is generally a good philosophy.

The order of "trust but verify" is also important. It starts with the word *trust*. When we trust someone or something, we are taking a risk. We risk that we will be disappointed or let down. We risk that our trust will have been misplaced, perhaps even abused. Trust is both an emotional and a logical act. When we trust someone we make ourselves vulnerable to them, and in some cases that can generate fear in us. That's an emotional reaction to trusting. So we use logic to consider the pros and cons of trusting the person or situation. We try to calculate the probability of gain and loss. Part of the logical reaction to trust is calculating the worst case scenarios. We ask ourselves to imagine the worst that can happen if we trust this person, and we try to mitigate our risks. We also look at past history or the person's track record to review how they handled our trust before. In the end, trust requires both logic and emotion.

We feel trust. Two of the most important emotions associated with trust are love and friendship. We are never hurt more than when our trust if violated by someone we love, or a friend. Psychology experts define trust in a number of different ways. They define trust in dimensions of predictability, value exchange, delayed reciprocity, and exposed vulnerabilities. Based on these four dimensions, they derive the following four definitions of trust:

> *Definition 1:* Trust means being able to predict what other people will do and what situations will occur. If we can surround ourselves with people we trust, then we can create a safe present and an even better future (predictability).

> *Definition 2:* Trust means making an exchange with someone when you do not have full knowledge about them, their intent and the things they are offering to you (value exchange).

> *Definition 3:* Trust means giving something now with an expectation that it will be repaid, possibly in some unspecified way at some unspecified time in the future (delayed reciprocity).

> *Definition 4:* Trust means enabling other people to take advantage of your vulnerabilities—but expecting that they will not do this (exposed vulnerabilities).

I am no psychology expert, but I see a pattern emerging when I look at these four definitions: trust requires me to work and worry. I have to work to figure out if I should trust someone or something, and then I have to worry if I will get value back now or later. I also have to worry about whether I will be taken advantage of. That's the nature of human trust. Fortunately, that's not the nature of God's trust.

The dimensions in God's definition of trust are different. They are: personal, perfect, and risk free.

Personal:

2 Samuel 7:27-29

²⁷ *O LORD Almighty, God of Israel, you have revealed this to your servant, saying, 'I will build a house for you.' So*

your servant has found courage to offer you this prayer. ²⁸ *O Sovereign LORD, you are God! Your words are trustworthy, and you have promised these good things to your servant.* ²⁹ *Now be pleased to bless the house of your servant, that it may continue forever in your sight; for you, O Sovereign LORD, have spoken, and with your blessing the house of your servant will be blessed forever.*

In this passage David is laying claim on God's personal promise to him. God promised He would build a house for David, His servant. And David, knowing that God's word is trustworthy, has full confidence that God will deliver on this promise. He does not need to verify or check the contract or read the fine print. God delivers. With God, trust is personal.

Perfect:

<u>Psalm 9:9-11</u>

⁹ *The LORD is a refuge for the oppressed, a stronghold in times of trouble.* ¹⁰ *Those who know your name will trust in you, for you, LORD, have never forsaken those who seek you.* ¹¹ *Sing praises to the LORD, enthroned in Zion; proclaim among the nations what He has done.*

I love this passage in the Bible. So often we feel like we need refuge from life's daily grind. Yet those who know God and trust in Him will never be forsaken. God has never failed; not once, not ever. All we need to do is seek Him and He will be there for us. Even in the times when we feel the loneliest and most abandoned, He is really there with us. I am reminded of the poem entitled *Footprints*:

One night a man had a dream. He dreamed he was walking along the beach with the LORD. Across the sky flashed scenes from his life. For each scene he noticed two sets of footprints in the sand. One belonging to him and the other to the LORD.

When the last scene of his life flashed before him, he looked back at the footprints in the sand. He noticed that many times along the path of his life there was only one set of footprints. He also noticed that it happened at the very lowest and saddest times of his life.

This really bothered him and he questioned the LORD about it. "LORD, you said that once I decided to follow you, you'd walk with me all the way. But I have noticed that during the most troublesome times in my life there is only one set of footprints. I don't understand why when I needed you most you would leave me"

The LORD replied, "My precious, precious child, I love you and I would never leave you! During your times of trial and suffering, when you see only one set of footprints, it was then that I carried you."

God has a perfect track record, and any trust we place in Him is a sure bet! He will never abandon us, and we can trust Him to carry us through the deepest valleys in our lives. Psalm 37 is another reminder of God's faithfulness and trustworthiness:

<u>Psalm 37:4-6</u>

⁴ Delight yourself in the LORD and He will give you the desires of your heart. ⁵ Commit your way to the LORD; trust in Him and He will do this: ⁶ He will make your righteousness shine like the dawn, the justice of your cause like the noonday sun.

Risk free:

<u>Proverbs 3:4-6</u>

⁴ Then you will win favor and a good name in the sight of God and man. ⁵ Trust in the LORD with all your heart

*and lean not on your own understanding; [6] in all your ways
acknowledge Him, and He will make your paths straight.*

With God we have the added benefit that we don't have to rely on our
strength, intelligence, and especially our own understanding. If we are
faithful enough to trust Him and acknowledge His sovereignty, He will
guide our paths and make them straight. There is no *quid pro quo* with
God. No "this for that." You can trust Him, and it costs you nothing.
Trusting God is risk free.

CHAPTER NINE

Be Humble

It's hard to think of a dog as being humble. To be humble implies that despite the fact that they know how skilled, educated or talented they are, a person chooses to keep a low profile about it. They don't boast about their skill or talent. Often times, in fact, they choose to minimize or at least try not to draw attention to themselves or gain recognition for it.

Strangely, the more a genuinely humble person attempts to stay out of the limelight, the more accolades they seem to get from the people around them. We like people who are humble. We think it's a good quality. Generally, we dislike people who demonstrate the opposite of humility: arrogance. A humble person is someone who is not high or lofty. They are not pretentious. They are unassuming. A humble person is not proud and doesn't think that they deserve special treatment. On the contrary, they consider themselves unworthy when judged by the demands of God. But if to be humble takes a sense of self-awareness, can Jag really be a humble dog? He sure acts like he understands the meaning of the word.

Jag never pretends to be someone or something he's not. He's comfortable in his own fur. He likes being a dog. I imagine that when he looks in the mirror, he's okay with the dog that stares back at him. He stands proud, but he is not prideful. He's confident, but he is not arrogant about it. He knows he is low dog on the totem pole at home. Jag understands that when it comes to the family pecking order, there's mom and dad, then big sister, then little sister, and then there's him. I think he's good with that. He shows deferential and sometimes submissive respect – a sign of a humble spirit. Jag is just happy to be a part of the family.

When you look up the word humble in *Webster's* dictionary, one of the ways it is defined is "marked by meekness." Meek is a word that is often misunderstood. It sounds lame. We've all heard the saying "meek as a mouse." Who really wants to be thought of as meek? I'm not sure where the word first got its bad rap. The reality is that the definition of meek is "humble in spirit or manner; suggesting mildness; modest; enduring injury with patience and without resentment; not violent; mild of temper; not easily provoked or irritated; not vain or haughty; forbearing."

Some definitions of the word meek also include "evidencing little spirit or courage; overly submissive or compliant; inclined or willing to submit to orders or wishes of others." I suspect it is these kinds of words that give "meek" a bad rap. However, I think this point of view would miss an important aspect of meekness.

To be meek does not mean to be weak! Meekness is not the absence of power; it's the controlling of power. Jag may be meek, but he is not without power. Sometimes Jag and I play rough. We wrestle each other and tumble around the floor a bit. I grab at him, and he paws at me. I try to pin him down, and he playfully bites my arms and hands. The key world is "playfully." Jag has the power to bite down hard enough to do some serious harm to my arm and hands, but he never does. He bites down just gently enough to make it fun and not painful. He controls his power. Moreover, I can tell him to stop and almost instantly, he stops. Jag is meek, but he's not without power. I think Jag really is a humble dog and I've learned the true meaning of the word by watching him.

It is not natural for a person to be humble. We are not born humble, thus it must be a learned behavior. A humble person learns to understand their life and they know what they are like. They learn not to be overly proud and they don't think they are the most important person in the world. However, a humble person is not the same as a weak person. They can be people of great strength of character, power and authority. The humble person trusts God with everything, now and in the future. The Bible tells us clearly how God feels about those who are humble.

Matthew 5:5

⁵*Blessed are the meek, for they will inherit the earth.*

<u>Psalm 149:3-5</u>

³*Let them praise His name with dancing and make music to Him with tambourine and harp. ⁴ For the LORD takes delight in His people; He crowns the humble with salvation. ⁵ Let the saints rejoice in this honor and sing for joy on their beds.*

<u>Matthew 18:3-5</u>

³*And He said: "I tell you the truth, unless you change and become like little children, you will never enter the kingdom of heaven. ⁴Therefore, whoever humbles himself like this child is the greatest in the kingdom of heaven. ⁵And whoever welcomes a little child like this in my name welcomes me."*

<u>Matthew 23:11-12</u>

¹¹*The greatest among you will be your servant. ¹²For whoever exalts himself will be humbled, and whoever humbles himself will be exalted.*

God gives humble men and women two thumbs up! In the end, I suspect it is the humble people who are the happiest. Lucky for me, Jag is teaching me what it means to be humble. I hope I have the strength and courage to be more humble each day.

CHAPTER TEN

Respect and Obey Your Master

Jag respects and obeys me. He allows himself to be vulnerable and follows my instructions without question. I believe it goes beyond simple obedience and respect; I think Jag also trusts me. Jag knows that I only have his best interest in mind. When I take him to the veterinarian, even though he does not like it, he allows himself to be prodded and poked. He submits to whatever we subject him to. He could run away or he could at least make it difficult to take care of him. Instead, he chooses to respect and obey me. Ultimately, Jag's obedience always works out best for him.

The Bible has much to say about obedience. The word obey appears hundreds of times throughout scripture. Here are just a few examples of its use:

Ephesians 6:4-6

> ⁴*Fathers, do not exasperate your children; instead, bring them up in the training and instruction of the Lord.* ⁵*Slaves, obey your earthly masters with respect and fear, and with sincerity of heart, just as you would obey Christ.* ⁶*Obey them not only to win their favor when their eye is on you, but like slaves of Christ, doing the will of God from your heart.*

<u>Colossians 3:21-23</u>

²¹*Fathers, do not embitter your children, or they will become discouraged.* ²²*Slaves, obey your earthly masters in everything; and do it, not only when their eye is on you and to win their favor, but with sincerity of heart and reverence for the Lord.* ²³*Whatever you do, work at it with all your heart, as working for the Lord, not for men.*

There's something interesting about the word obey. Performing a Google search on the word obey reveals two primary types of information. There is a great deal of material on dog obedience and there are thousands of references to obedience in the religious sense. It seems to me that the word obey is not one we like very much in our culture. It has a restrictive feeling to it. We have to obey the laws. That means we can't just do whatever we want all the time.

Children and young adults are warned to obey their parents or suffer the consequences. We are instructed to obey our teachers because no matter how mean they are to us, they know best. Even the verses in Ephesians and Colossians refer to slaves obeying their masters. We certainly don't think of ourselves as slaves. Most of us want to exercise our free will and don't want anyone to tell us what we should or shouldn't do.

What is obedience? Webster says that obedience is the act or habit of obeying; submission, and compliance. Put another way, it means to comply with commands and to submit to authority. The majority of us generally accept having to obey traffic laws and other rules established by our society. We realize that most of these rules are in place to keep us safe. Still, down deep we all have a bit of rebellion in us that tends to resist the concept of obedience. We start exercising that tendency from a very early age. Any parent of a two-year old child can explain the concept of rebellion and disobedience quite well. They don't call that age the "terrible twos" for nothing.

The Bible teaches us to be obedient. Importantly it points out the penalty for disobedience. In the context of the gospel of Jesus Christ, to obey means to comply with God's will, to live in accordance with His teachings and the promptings of His Spirit, and to keep His commandments. That's easier said than done!

The best reason to obey is simply because God commands it:

<u>John 14:15</u>

¹⁵*If you love me, you will obey what I command.*

However, God gives us free will to grow spiritually, and He does not require unwilling compliance or blind obedience to Him. Rather as we mature in our faith, we learn the real reasons why obedience is the right course of action in our lives. The most obvious reasons to obey are the consequences of disobedience. When we disobey we dramatically improve our chances for suffering. Whether we disobey the civil law or God's laws, the penalties are always painful.

Disobedience has a *quid pro quo* associated with it. If you break the law by drinking and driving you will go to jail – if you get caught. If you cheat on an exam in class you will fail the class – if you get caught. If you lie to your parents you will get grounded – if you get caught. If you cheat on your spouse you will end up in divorce court – if you get caught. But what if we don't get caught? Is there a penalty for disobedience if the act goes undetected?

There is indeed a price of disobedience even if we don't get caught. First, let's not forget that we cannot hide anything from God. Thus our behavior is never truly hidden. Secondly, as we engage in active disobedience, we develop habits. These habits can lead us to believe that we are above the law and somehow immune to it. So we continue to disobey and even become more blatant in our defiance.

Evidence of this is not hard to find. We need only look at examples of some of our political leaders who have been exposed for having extramarital affairs. We are shocked and amazed to find out that in some cases these individuals had been engaging in this behavior for years! That means they were not caught the first time. Maybe they were not caught the second, third, or fourth time. However, eventually they became brazen about it, perhaps even carelessly thinking that they were immune to being exposed. The next thing we see is the devastating effects on the individual and his entire family. Disobedience carries a huge price.

Ultimately disobedience can open the door to a spirit of rebellion. Unless we confess our sin and repent, it can lead to a hardening of the heart. And that carries its own risks. Consider the price that Pharaoh paid when his heart was hardened despite Moses' warnings and the plagues that God sent. Pharaoh stayed steadfast in his disobedience. It eventually cost him the life of his firstborn son. That's a pretty hefty price to pay for disobedience. The special sting of disobedience really hits full force when we recognize that the penalties we suffer are those we've brought upon ourselves.

But the threat of penalties is not the most compelling reason for us to live a life of obedience. Instead, it's all about the rewards. God blesses those who are obedient.

<u>Deuteronomy 28:1-3</u>

> [1] *If you fully obey the LORD your God and carefully follow all His commands I give you today, the LORD your God will set you high above all the nations on earth.* [2] *All these blessings will come upon you and accompany you if you obey the LORD your God:* [3] *You will be blessed in the city and blessed in the country.*

When we walk on God's path and live according to His will, we enjoy the many blessings He has for us.

CHAPTER ELEVEN

Allow Yourself to be Cared For

A few years ago we almost lost Jag after he had an operation. The complications that occurred post operatively were serious enough that for many days we were not sure if he would survive. Our family rejoiced when Jag began to show improvement. After ten days we were able to bring him home, where we continued to care for him until he was able to make a full recovery.

Anyone who has had the experience of taking care of an ill loved one knows how difficult that can be. It is especially difficult if the person needing the care does not cooperate in the process. During his recovery, we had to fuss over Jag. We had to manage his wound to make sure it did not become infected. No doubt that must have been uncomfortable for him. We had to give him medication; it was clear that he did not enjoy that either. To keep him from licking his wound, we had to place a plastic cone around his head that made it terribly uncomfortable for him to lie down. To make sure he did not continue to lose weight, we had to insist that he eat solid foods and drink water when all he wanted was to be left alone.

Through this entire process, I noticed two things about Jag. First, he allowed us to take care of him. Despite the fact that we were causing him pain and discomfort, he trusted us and let us watch over him. Secondly, he was always grateful. We could see it in his eyes. He also thanked us with a gentle wag of his tail whenever he could muster it. Jag got better, but in the process he healed us, too. He healed us from the guilt we felt for putting him in harms way. What was supposed to be a simple routine procedure had turned into a life threatening nightmare for Jag. We agonized over the fact that we had caused him such pain and discomfort, and we were horrified to think that we might actually lose him. But through it all, his eyes and his wagging tail told us, "It's okay; I know you only had my best interests at heart." Jag may have allowed us to take care of him, but in the process, he also took care of us.

Two of my favorite stories in the Bible are when Jesus heals the paralytic man and the second is when He raised Lazarus.

Mark 2:1-12

> [1]*A few days later, when Jesus again entered Capernaum, the people heard that He had come home.* [2]*So many gathered that there was no room left, not even outside the door, and He preached the word to them.* [3]*Some men came, bringing to Him a paralytic, carried by four of them.* [4]*Since they could not get him to Jesus because of the crowd, they made an opening in the roof above Jesus and, after digging through it, lowered the mat the paralyzed man was lying on.* [5]*When Jesus saw their faith, He said to the paralytic, "Son, your sins are forgiven."*

> [6]*Now some teachers of the law were sitting there, thinking to themselves,* [7]*"Why does this fellow talk like that? He's blaspheming! Who can forgive sins but God alone?"*

> [8]*Immediately Jesus knew in His spirit that this was what they were thinking in their hearts, and He said to them, "Why are you thinking these things?* [9]*Which is easier: to say to the paralytic, 'Your sins are forgiven,' or to say, 'Get up, take your mat and walk'?* [10]*But that you may know that the Son of Man has authority on earth to forgive sins…"* He said to the paralytic, [11]*"I tell you, get up, take your mat and go home."* [12]*He got up, took his mat and walked out in full view of them all. This amazed everyone and they praised God, saying, "We have never seen anything like this!"*

Now those are some good friends! They wanted to take care of their friend so much that they went through a great deal of trouble to get him before the Lord. Their faith that Jesus could heal their friend drove them to take whatever action was needed. They were even willing to make a hole in the roof of a stranger's house! No doubt, they must have been prepared to pay for the damage.

Jesus did heal the man but something even more important took place. All who were there witnessed the awesome power of Jesus, and they believed. So who was really healed? Was it the paralytic or his friends? The answer is both!

When Lazarus became sick, Martha did her best to take care of him. Certainly she must have tried every medical treatment available to her at that time to save her brother. No doubt she relied on prayers as well. Yet Lazarus died. It happens every day. People get sick and despite our best efforts and our prayers, sometimes they die.

John 11:1-7

¹Now a man named Lazarus was sick. He was from Bethany, the village of Mary and her sister Martha. ²This Mary, whose brother Lazarus now lay sick, was the same one who poured perfume on the Lord and wiped His feet with her hair. ³So the sisters sent word to Jesus, "Lord, the one you love is sick."

⁴When He heard this, Jesus said, "This sickness will not end in death. No, it is for God's glory so that God's Son may be glorified through it." ⁵Jesus loved Martha and her sister and Lazarus. ⁶Yet when He heard that Lazarus was sick, He stayed where He was two more days. ⁷Then He said to His disciples, "Let us go back to Judea."

John 11:11-15

¹¹After He had said this, He went on to tell them, "Our friend Lazarus has fallen asleep; but I am going there to wake him up." ¹²His disciples replied, "Lord, if he sleeps, he will get better." ¹³Jesus had been speaking of his death, but His disciples thought He meant natural sleep. ¹⁴So then He told them plainly, "Lazarus is dead, ¹⁵and for your sake I am glad I was not there, so that you may believe. But let us go to him."

John 11:37-39

³⁷But some of them said, "Could not He who opened the eyes of the blind man have kept this man from dying?" ³⁸Jesus, once more deeply moved, came to the tomb. It was a cave with a stone laid across the entrance. ³⁹"Take away the stone," He said. "But, Lord," said Martha, the sister of the dead man, "by this time there is a bad odor, for he has been there four days." ⁴⁰Then Jesus said, "Did I not tell you that if you believed, you would see the glory of God?" ⁴¹So they took away the stone. Then Jesus looked up and said, "Father, I thank you that you have heard me. ⁴²I knew that you always hear me, but I said this for the benefit of the people standing here, that they may believe that you sent me."

⁴³When He had said this, Jesus called in a loud voice, "Lazarus, come out!" ⁴⁴The dead man came out, his hands and feet wrapped with strips of linen, and a cloth around his face. Jesus said to them, "Take off the grave clothes and let him go."

What a great story! I love the humanity that Jesus shows in this passage. He wept for his friend Lazarus. Jesus could have shown up days before to heal His friend before he died. He could have just wished it from where He was without even making the trip to see Lazarus. Instead He used this occasion to demonstrate the power God has over life and death. I can only imagine what Lazarus must have thought after he came out of the tomb. Do you think he said, "Well it's about time you got here, Jesus! I was starting to rot in there." No, there can be no doubt that Lazarus bowed down before Jesus and worshiped Him. Lazarus was the ultimate sick patient; he was dead! Yet his healer brought him back to life and in doing so healed not just him but everyone else who witnessed the miracle.

When we are sick, we should allow others to take care of us. By doing so we help them as much as they help us.

CHAPTER TWELVE

Play Often

In his article published by the American Academy of Pediatrics titled *The Importance of Play in Promoting Healthy Child Development and Maintaining Strong Parent-Child Bonds*, Dr. Kenneth R. Ginsburg wrote the following in his abstract:

> Play is essential to development because it contributes to the cognitive, physical, social, and emotional well-being of children and youth. Play also offers an ideal opportunity for parents to engage fully with their children. Despite the benefits derived from play for both children and parents, time for free play has been markedly reduced for some children. This report addresses a variety of factors that have reduced play, including a hurried lifestyle, changes in family structure, and increased attention to academics and enrichment activities at the expense of recess or free child-centered play. This report offers guidelines on how pediatricians can advocate for children by helping families, school systems, and communities consider how best to ensure that play is protected as they seek the balance in children's lives to create the optimal developmental milieu.

Clearly playing is important to child development. Yet at some point in our lives, we stop playing. We grow up and suddenly playing has no place in our lives. The cruelest of ironies is this: those who have the most money buy the most toys, yet they have the least amount of time to play with them. Take a walk in a marina and admire the biggest, most luxurious yachts tied to the dock. It's those same yachts that sit there idle, never being used. Their rich owners are too busy to make time for a boat ride.

I don't need to go to a marina to witness this sad waste of toys. All I had to do was go into my own basement. We were blessed to live in a very comfortable house. Downstairs was a virtual playground. We had a ping pong table, a foosball table, an air hockey table and a pool table. There was a television complete with DVD player and a video game console. We probably had a dozen game boards we bought to keep us busy on rainy days. We were indeed blessed. Still are! Yet most of these items sat quietly collecting dust, rarely being used by anyone in the family. And ironically, there were many times when we were sitting in the living room on a Saturday afternoon, and someone will inevitably declare, "I'm bored." I am willing to bet this happens in your family also. We've since moved to a smaller house in California. We have no basement, so there is no room for all the toys. We found better homes for them before we moved. I hope the family that has them is using them to bring the family together and actually play!

What happened to our sense of creativity and imagination? Remember when you were a kid? You could entertain yourself for hours with an empty box. Remember those rare (but awesome!) days when you were lucky enough to get an empty box of something as large as a refrigerator? We made those into space ships! And we traveled throughout the galaxy landing on planets and facing all sorts of hideous monsters, ultimately returning safely to our home planet as heroes. We played so hard and for so many hours that our moms would have to call us three times before we were finally able to tear ourselves away from our play and go inside for dinner. We had no GameBoys or Wii video game consoles. We had no Internet, no Facebook or My Space on which to waste hours each day. There was no such thing as cell phones for us to send mindless text messages for hours at a time. We created a virtual world using nothing more than our imaginations, and we played.

Today, at least here in the United States, even simple playtime has become complicated. We have to plan "play dates" for our children to get together. Whereas years ago a spontaneous game of football or soccer could break out at any moment in the school yard or the open field behind someone's home, now we have organized leagues with all the high pressure of professional sports. These organized games also come with insanely intense, stressed-out parents yelling from the sidelines as their kids try to "play" the game. The spaces beneath the Christmas trees are littered with dozens of boxes filled with sophisticated toys to help entertain our children. There is nothing more humorous than watching a three-year old rip open a Christmas gift and be more entertained playing with the box than the item that was in it! What have we done to the concept of playing?

Jag loves to play, even now that he is nearly twelve years old – more than eighty in dog years. He may move slower these days and he may not be able to play for long without taking a break, but he still loves to play. Moreover, he plays with the same innocence as he did when he was a puppy. I've nicknamed him Linus, in honor of the *Peanuts* character who is constantly walking around with a security blanket. Jag has a security blanket, too, and he carries it in his mouth from room to room. When it's time to play, Jag brings his blanket and challenges one of us to a game of tug of war – his favorite game of all time. He almost always gets someone to take him up on his offer. Two things happen when we play with Jag: first, we always have a good time and a good laugh to go along with it. Second, he wins every match because he can outlast any of us. He plays until someone else quits first!

The benefits of playing are many. Playing promotes the use of our imaginations and it helps reduce our stress levels. For children it has the added benefit of promoting language and communication skills, as well as a healthy understanding of the importance of social interaction.

Consider this verse from Zechariah:

Zechariah 8:4-5

[4] *This is what the LORD Almighty says: "Once again men and women of ripe old age will sit in the streets of Jerusalem, each with cane in hand because of his age.* [5] *The city streets will be filled with boys and girls playing there."*

This verse creates a mental image for me of what our lives can be like if we stop playing. We will become men and women of ripe old age sitting around with canes in our hands while around us kids will be at play. Jag is eighty four years old. If a game breaks out, he lifts his old bones and joins in the fun. Regardless of our years, we should always nurture our ability and desire to play. When I die, I hope I die playing rather than sitting on a rocking chair lamenting the lost "good old days." Get up and play.

CHAPTER THIRTEEN

Don't Complain

I personally believe we developed language because of our deep inner need to complain. ~Jane Wagner

What was the first thing Adam told God? "Everything here is too perfect." So God created Eve. What was the first thing Eve said to God? "Everything would have been perfect if you had not created *him*."

The joke works best if you add a healthy dose of whining to your voice when telling it. It seems that we are hardwired to complain, and society accommodates the whiner in us at every turn. Our entire system of justice is based on complaints. Every major company has a department dedicated to complaints; they call it customer service now. Funny thing is that if we had gotten good customer service in the first place, they would not need a customer service department. Ironic.

Jag doesn't complain. Every morning we open the sliding glass door to the deck and let Jag out. He sniffs around the backyard for a bit, takes care of his business, and makes his way back up the steps of the deck and stands just outside the glass door. He does not bark, he does not whine. He just stands there and patiently waits until someone opens the door for him. I will admit that there are times when I forget to let him back in. After a while, when I finally notice Jag's not around, I run to the door. That's where I find him, just sitting or lying down, waiting. He wags his tail as if to say, "There you are, Dad; I've been waiting for you!" He's not mad, he's not irritated. He's just happy to be let back in. He does not complain and he does not retreat to a corner holding a grudge against me.

I, of course, feel terrible, but he does not let me feel that way for long. Jag is not a complainer. I wish that were true for the rest of us.

The truth is, for some reason many of us simply like to complain! Here's another interesting factoid about complaining: those who have the most, complain the most. When I was in Haiti on a short term mission trip, I was impressed by the poverty and need that was all around me. So many people there live in conditions that are simply subhuman. There's garbage everywhere – not because the Haitians are dirty people; on the contrary. The reason there is garbage everywhere is because the nation has no infrastructure to properly manage waste. Very few roads outside the main city of Port Au Prince are paved. Most are nothing more than rocky and bumpy trails that can only be navigated on foot. Pigs, chickens, donkeys, horses, bulls and cows share the same drinking and bathing water as the villagers. It's heartbreaking.

As we traveled the countryside and visited the poorest of villages, I heard many things. But what I did not hear was complaining. The people of Haiti, despite their extremely difficult circumstances, were glad to have what little they did have. They were especially grateful to receive whatever help was offered. They did not have much, so I guess that left them little to complain about.

Immediately upon my return to the United States from Haiti I was smacked squarely on the face with the stark contrast in attitude between "the haves" and "the have nots." Our flight from Haiti had just landed in Miami, and as I waited in the airport for my connecting flight I realized that I had a craving for a Burger King Whopper. I wanted it done *my way*. So I went to the airport's Burger King and patiently waited my turn in line to order my lunch. As I stood at the counter and ordered my food, a burly, red-faced man stomped up beside me and began yelling at the young woman behind the register who was taking my order. He was clearly not happy. Apparently his burger had onions, and he had specifically ordered it without onions. The guy was livid. He ranted for what seemed like minutes. I looked on feeling ashamed and saddened. I was ashamed that in my country, one of my fellow citizens could be so idiotic, so insensitive, and such a spoiled whiner. I immediately thought of the people I had left behind in Haiti just a few hours earlier. They would have been thrilled to have that burger, with or without onions! I can't imagine they would have complained about it at all. I suppose they would have simply taken the onions off the burger and set them aside – or more likely offered them to someone else. But I am sure they would not have wasted any time or energy complaining about it. No, it seems complaining is done best by those who have the most.

Author Franklin P. Jones once said, "Untold suffering seldom is." He was right. Complaining about what we are suffering is natural. For Americans it seems we consider it a God given right. It's the nature of complaining; we love to share it. There are a few interesting qualities that make the art of complaining fascinating. Let's consider some of them:

1. Very often we create the very issue that we complain about.

   I will not be as those who spend the day in complaining of headache, and the night in drinking the wine that gives it. ~Johann Wolfgang von Goethe

2. When we have nothing to complain about, we make it up.

   The people who live in a golden age usually go around complaining how yellow everything looks. ~Randall Jarrell

3. When there is doubt if we lack intellect, we open our mouths and provide all the necessary evidence.

   The tendency to whining and complaining may be taken as the surest sign symptom of little souls and inferior intellects. ~Lord Jeffrey

4. We complain even when we get a gift!

   People that pay for things never complain. It's the guy you give something to that you can't please. ~Will Rogers

5. We tend to focus on the negative rather than the positive.

   Instead of complaining that the rosebush is full of thorns, be happy that the thorn bush has roses. ~Proverb

Alexander Kjerulf, author of *Happy Hour is 9 to 5: A Practical Guide to Making Yourself and Others Happy at Work*, also authored an article entitled *Top 10 Reasons Why Constant Complaining is So Toxic in the Workplace*. Here is his list:

- It makes things look worse than they are
- It becomes a habit
- You get what you focus on
- It leads to "onedownmanship"
- It makes people despondent
- It kills innovation
- It favors negative people
- It promotes bad relationships
- It creates cliques
- Pessimism is bad for you

That's a great list. I am convinced that they apply equally as well in our personal lives as they do in the professional setting. If the first nine points don't convince you that complaining is a bad thing, maybe the last one will. Psychologist Martin Seligman showed in his groundbreaking research in positive psychology that people who see the world in a positive light have a long list of advantages. They live longer, they are healthier, they have more friends and better social lives, they enjoy life more and they are more successful at work. I guess we can live longer and happier lives if we just stop complaining!

Here's what God has to say about complaining:

Philippians 2:13-15

> [13] *for it is God who works in you to will and to act according to His good purpose.* [14] *Do everything without complaining or arguing,* [15] *so that you may become blameless and pure, children of God without fault in a crooked and depraved generation, in which you shine like stars in the universe*

I wonder if there will be a sign hanging on the wall in God's office in heaven that says "no whining". Philippians 2:13-15 seems to indicate so.

CHAPTER FOURTEEN

Don't Dwell on Yesterday and Don't Worry About Tomorrow

In life there are many things that are in our control. We can control what we choose to spend our time on and who we spend it with. We control our thoughts and the actions we take. We can control how we spend our money. No doubt we can each make a long list of items that are firmly in our control. It would not be difficult to make an even longer list of the things in life that are not in our control. Two of the most obvious things that are not in our control are what happened yesterday and what's going to happen tomorrow.

As far as I can tell, Jag has never concerned himself with what happened yesterday. No doubt he remembers it. How do we know he remembers yesterday? Yvette and I usually sit to watch the evening news and some of the political talk shows. Invariably around 9:00 p.m., almost like clockwork, Jag comes over to us. If he could talk we know he would be saying something like this: "It's time for my snack. Please come with me to the kitchen. I need your help." Since he is obviously unable to speak, he uses body language to make his needs understood. He wags his tail and responds enthusiastically when we tease him, asking him, "What do you want little boy?" He literally motions us to the kitchen and insists that we follow him.

When we get to the kitchen, Jag points to the refrigerator where he knows we keep his beloved watermelon. We usually hide his medication in the first piece of watermelon that we give him; he knows we do it and frankly he doesn't care. He just wants the watermelon. There are many other examples that have convinced us that Jag remembers yesterday. One thing is sure however – he does not dwell on it.

If Jag does not dwell on yesterday, he couldn't care less about tomorrow. He's not concerned about whether it's going to rain or if there is going to be a thunderstorm. He does not worry about whether he will have food and shelter. Many reading this will be tempted to believe that Jag does not worry about tomorrow because he's a dog, and dogs are not self-aware, thus they don't have a sense of time – of past, present or future. Indeed, that may be true. Another possibility is that Jag is not worried about the future because he realizes he can't control it and because he trusts us to take care of him come what may. And that's the primary lesson we need to learn from Jag when it comes to dwelling on the past or worrying about the future: they are both futile and unnecessary activities.

The past has two undeniable qualities about it. First, every past event is uniquely its own and different from all others. Second, the past is undeniably unchangeable. Events in the past are uniquely different from any other event ever before it or any event that will occur in the future. Nothing can be repeated precisely as it was in the past. No matter how similar it may seem, a past event is just that: a past event. Thus it is illogical to try to re-live the past. Yet that's what many of us do. We try desperately to hang on to events that occurred in the past, and we try even more desperately to have them repeat. Moreover, given the fact that past events are unchangeable, it seems foolish to spend any time worrying about them.

There are some things we should do with the past, though. We should remember the happy times fondly, and be grateful to have had them. And we should learn from our past experiences to improve our chances of repeating success and avoiding failures in the future.

Jesus offered this advice when it comes to worrying about our lives:

Matthew 6:25-26

[25]*Therefore I tell you, do not worry about your life, what you will eat or drink; or about your body, what you will wear. Is not life more important than food, and the body more important than clothes?* [26]*Look at the birds of the air;*

they do not sow or reap or store away in barns, and yet your heavenly Father feeds them. Are you not much more valuable than they?

Some may be tempted to look at this passage as an excuse to do nothing to help themselves grow personally or professionally. They might interpret Jesus' message to say that we should not think about planning for our future or strive to do our best in our professional and personal lives. A few would point to this passage as proof that saving for retirement is unnecessary because the Lord says not to worry about it. Those individuals would all be reading this passage with the wrong-colored filters.

The Bible also says this:

Genesis 2:15

The LORD God took the man and put him in the Garden of Eden to work it and take care of it.

Proverbs 10:4

Lazy hands make a man poor, but diligent hands bring wealth.

Jeremiah 29:11

"For I know the plans I have for you," declares the LORD, "plans to prosper you and not to harm you, plans to give you hope and a future."

God does not want us to worry about things or focus our attention on building shrines to ourselves. The house we live in, the cars we drive, the clothes we wear, the toys we have – all such things as these are not to be our primary concerns. God expects us to work. He expects us to be diligent and to use the talents He has bestowed upon us for good. He has plans for us; plans for us to prosper and to have hope for the future. But His plan includes us living and walking in His path and being faithful to "working the plan" rather than constantly complaining about it.

CHAPTER FIFTEEN

Be Sorry When You Pee On the Rug

Every once in a while Jag has an accident and he urinates on the rug. Sometimes it happens because we were out of the house too long and he was unable to hold it. Other times it happens because of a side effect of his allergy medication. The medication makes him thirsty and increases his need to pee. Each time it happens two things take place. First, we usually get a bit upset. After all, who wants to have to clean up dog pee from their carpets? The second thing that happens is that Jag shows us he is sorry.

If Jag has the accident while we are out of the house, we know something is wrong as soon as we walk through the door because he greets us somberly. Normally he would be happy to see us and he would be whimpering with joy. But if he comes to us slowly with his head held low, we know something bad has happened. Like a little boy riddled with guilt and shame, he takes us to the scene of the crime. If he could speak he would be screaming, "I did it, okay? There, I admit it. It was me. I peed on the rug. But you should not have left me here alone all this time! You know what that medicine does to me!"

We can't stay angry with Jag very long. It's hard to stay angry with someone who is clearly sorry for what he did and does not try to hide it or lie about it. Imagine what the world would be like if people would be genuinely sorry when they did something wrong and their actions clearly indicated their remorse. It would change the face of our entire political system! How refreshing would it be if some of our political leaders would take a lesson from Jag and simply be sorry when they pee on the rug?

It is part of the human condition to offend and to be offended. The truth is that at some point in our lives, we will all do something that we should be sorry for. It is equally true that at some point in our lives someone will do something to us for which they should be sorry. In fact, the chances are good that it will happen many times, over and over. That's why the apology was invented. An apology makes it possible for us to live together and strive for a common good.

An apology has a healing power to it. All healing of emotional wounds begins with an apology. Without the healing powers of apology, we would succumb to our impulse to seek revenge. We would continue to feud and hold grudges and we would continue other hostile behaviors that do nothing except add stress to our lives.

Charlene Laino wrote an article entitled *Health Benefits of a Sincere Apology*. In it, Laino argues that apologizing is potent medicine for both the giver and the receiver. The article, reviewed by Dr. Michael W. Smith, was featured on WebMD. Below is an excerpt of her article:

> *You gossiped and the person found out. You helped yourself to something that wasn't yours (such as someone's spouse). You stole. You lied. You read your child's diary. It never sits quite right -- you toss, you turn in bed, you have that sinking feeling in your chest, you eat, you drink too much, you get headaches.*

> *Carol Orsborn, PhD, a research associate at UCLA and author of 15 books including* Nothing Left Unsaid: Words to Help You and Your Loved Ones Through the Hardest Times *and* The Silver Pearl: Our Generation's Journey to Wisdom, *tells WebMD about a woman she met while writing the latter book.*

> *Barbara, age 50, was going through a divorce and her brother was her mainstay, talking her through lonely nights on the phone. Then she met the man of her dreams and moved away. She got so swept up in her new life; she put her brother on the backburner. She missed his birthday.*

> *That's when the sleepless nights began. She was embarrassed*

to even call. She knew he would be hurt -- but would he be angry? Eventually, she picked up the phone. Yes, he was hurt, but he said he understood. She started sleeping again -- and talking to her brother."[1]

I am sure we can all appreciate Charlene's point. When we behave in ways that we know we shouldn't, it affects us emotionally and physically. We eat too much and we stop exercising. We get headaches and we even lose sleep. What is the best medicine for ailments like these? The answer is a humble apology. I guess it is true; we sleep best when we have a clear conscience.

An apology meets the needs of both the person who has been mistreated and the person who needs to accept responsibility for doing the mistreating. For those on the receiving end of the apology, it can help soothe hurt feelings, melt away resentment, restore broken relationships and even heal broken hearts. Nothing bad comes from receiving a heartfelt, genuine apology. The benefits are no less significant for the offender. When we apologize, we acknowledge that we were wrong. Apologizing can be a very humbling experience that reminds us that we are not perfect. It does not mean that we don't need to pay a price or somehow make retribution for what we did wrong, but it allows us to also begin the healing process.

What keeps us from apologizing? More often than not the answer is our stubbornness and our arrogance. The price we pay when we hold on to our arrogance and refuse to admit it when we are wrong is very high. Arrogance breeds contempt, contempt breeds stupidity, and stupidity breeds disaster. We can all think of examples of individuals who have lost their careers, social status, wealth and even marriages because they were unable to apologize and take responsibility for some action. By contrast, when we are able to apologize we become vulnerable and others may become empathetic with us. When we offer a sincere apology, we release others to forgive us. We also benefit from the fact that we will be seen as what we are: a fallible human being. In the end, apologizing keeps us connected to our families and friends, and it leads us toward healthier relationships.

---

1   Laino, Charlene. "Health Benefits of a Sincere Apology." WebMD. 15 October 2009 http://women.webmd.com/guide/health-benefits-of-sincere-apology.

There is one other very important lesson I've learned from Jag about being sorry and apologizing. Jag never pays back wrong with wrong. There have been times when I was in a foul mood and I said some harsh words to Jag. He has never turned around and peed on the carpet just to spite me. Jag must have read what God has to say on the subject:

1 Thessalonians 5:14-16

¹⁴And we urge you, brothers, warn those who are idle, encourage the timid, help the weak, be patient with everyone. ¹⁵Make sure that nobody pays back wrong for wrong, but always try to be kind to each other and to everyone else. ¹⁶Be joyful always.

We must not repay a wrong with a wrong. That's contrary to almost every human instinct. When we are treated poorly or unfairly, or if we are insulted, our first impulse is to pay back our offender with a dose of the same. Yet that is not what we are commanded to do. Instead, we are commanded to forgive:

Matthew 18:21-22

²¹Then Peter came to Jesus and asked, "Lord, how many times shall I forgive my brother when he sins against me? Up to seven times?" ²²Jesus answered, "I tell you, not seven times, but seventy-seven times."

Turning the other cheek is hard to do. But that's exactly what we must do. Note that Jesus did not say that we should wait for an apology to come before forgiving someone who has hurt us! We are to forgive even if the offender hasn't yet asked us to. Forgiving someone is more for our own benefit than it is for theirs. When we forgive someone, we are healed and released from any burden of guilt. Whether we are forgiving or apologizing, it feels good to take the load off our minds.

CHAPTER SIXTEEN

Ask for Help When You are Afraid

I enjoy watching and listening to a good thunderstorm. I'm the kind of person that sits and counts the seconds between the lightning strike and the sound of thunder to estimate how far the storm is from me. We probably all remember being taught to count the number of seconds between when you see the lightning and hear the thunder. Then take the number of seconds and divide by five, and that will tell you how far away the storm is in miles. For example, if you count ten seconds between the lightning and the thunder, the storm is two miles away. It's fun to do this, but only if you happen to be in a safe place, like inside your home. It's not as much fun if you are hiking on a mountain trail or out on an open field. Thunderstorms can be frightening.

Jag does not like thunderstorms. Noise phobia, often manifested as excessive fear during thunderstorms, is a relatively common affliction of dogs, and Jag is no exception. His sensitive ears detect thunderstorms long before ours do. He's as good as having a barometer in the house; we always know when a storm is coming because Jag gets increasingly restless. He definitely has a phobia of thunderstorms.

Fear is classified as a phobia when it is out of proportion to the danger of the real situation. Jag's fear of the thunderstorm certainly seems to be an overreaction relative to the danger it poses to him. I've explained that to him many times. But he doesn't care about my scientific explanation of the low probability of a lightning strike – he just wants to be protected. So as the storm approaches, regardless of time of day or night, Jag makes his way close to his mom or dad. Sometimes he comes to us trembling in fear and completely vulnerable.

I did some research to try to find a remedy that would help Jag overcome his phobia of thunderstorms. I was amazed at the number of potential treatments to help dogs with thunderstorm phobia. There are natural remedies, homeopathic remedies, flower essences, pharmaceutical solutions, music therapy, and my favorite: hug therapy.

An article in *The Whole Dog Journal* reported that Dr. Nicholas Dodman and his colleague Dr. Linda Aronson of the behavioral section at Tufts New England Veterinary Medical Center had been looking for something that would help reduce canine thunderstorm phobias when they discovered research papers on the effect of melatonin, an over-the-counter hormone used by humans to treat insomnia. Drs. Dodman and Aronson wondered whether melatonin might work on noise phobic dogs. As it turns out they discovered that there is some evidence to suggest that in fact, melatonin does help reduce anxiety and severe thunder phobia in dogs.

Other more "sophisticated" remedies include the use of Phosphorous PHUS 30C, which is available in health food stores. This is a natural compound which is used for fear of thunder or loud noises. If that doesn't work, according to experts, individual flower essences can also be used to address a wide range of discrete emotional imbalances. Remedies are matched to the specific mental and emotional needs of the animal. For dogs resistant to behavior modification, anxiety reducing drugs may offer a solution. The two traditionally used tranquilizers for noise phobia are Acepromazine and Valium.

Some believe that sedation may be the only way to help a dog with noise phobias. However, those who don't want to turn their dogs into junkies can try harp music. Yes, harp music. Apparently some tests suggest that the vibrations and blended tones of the harp have a relaxing effect on wolves, dogs, cats, monkeys, goats, sheep, donkeys and gorillas. Excellent news for gorilla lovers! I guess by now you can tell that I am not a huge fan of these artificial treatments.

My favorite type of therapy to help calm dogs suffering from thunder phobia is hug therapy. When I first was doing the research on it, I incorrectly assumed that it was exactly what it sounded like: hugs for my dog! It turns out that it actually refers to "body wrapping" and it seems to calm and focus some anxious and stressed dogs. Neurobiologists believe that any type of trauma can damage nerve receptors, leading to exaggerated responses to stimuli. By applying constantly maintained pressure, a wrap provides an unchanging, quieting stimulus that causes the receptors to adapt and modify their thresholds in a cumulative manner. Who would have thought? All I really had to do is wrap Jag in some plastic wrap and all his troubles would be over!

Joking aside, this therapy does make sense to me. We all benefit from a hug. Dog behaviorists have developed a variety of techniques for "wrapping" a dog ranging from T-shirts to elastic bandage wraps to give them that feeling of a consistent, secure hug. They use a sturdy, stretchy vest that hugs the torso like a body stocking. I've not invested in one for Jag yet. For now, we rely on the old fashioned kind of hug – we open our arms and give it, naturally and warmly. So when Jag comes to us afraid because of the thunder, we hug him and make him feel safe. Lo and behold, he's fine after that!

Here's the point: Jag knows to ask for help when he's afraid or any other time he needs it. He may not know about all the different solutions that we could offer him. He really doesn't care about all the "treatment options." He only knows that he needs one thing: to be comforted and to be reassured that all is going to be okay. Sometimes, that's exactly the same thing we need from God. We just need to know that we're going to be okay and that God will take care of us when we are afraid and need help.

Jesus Christ promised us that we would have a counselor and comforter. He encourages us not be afraid.

John 14:26-28

> [26]*But the Counselor, the Holy Spirit, whom the Father will send in my name, will teach you all things and will remind you of everything I have said to you.* [27]*Peace I leave with you; my peace I give you. I do not give to you as the world gives. Do not let your hearts be troubled and do not be afraid.* [28]*You heard me say, 'I am going away and I am coming back to you.' If you loved me, you would be glad that I am going to the Father, for the Father is greater than I.*

God also promises that He will rescue us and protect us. He will deliver us from our trouble.

<u>Psalm 91:13-15</u>

[13] *You will tread upon the lion and the cobra; you will trample the great lion and the serpent.* [14] *"Because he loves me," says the LORD, "I will rescue him; I will protect him, for he acknowledges my name.* [15] *He will call upon me, and I will answer him; I will be with him in trouble, I will deliver him and honor him.*

Jag's phobia of thunder has helped me learn more about how to ask for help when I need it or when I am afraid. We all go through thunderstorms in our lives, but we need not weather them alone. We have family and friends, and most importantly, a God that will see us through every time. We have nothing to fear! God is with us, yesterday, today and tomorrow.

EPILOGUE

Judge Advocate General, that's his name. Will he go to heaven when he dies? If there are dogs in heaven – and I sure hope there are – then Jag will certainly be there. From the moment he was born he has loved life and lived it to its fullest. He knows how to play, when to ask for help, how to give love, and when to be quiet. Jag has showered each of us with unconditional love and he has made us laugh until we cried. Jag trusts us. He has never worried about yesterday or tomorrow, and he has protected us whenever he thought we needed protecting. He's been a good and loyal friend, and I have learned much from him.

As you read the final few words of this short book, let it serve as a reminder to you as it has to me. Let us live our lives according to simple and profound Christian principles that keep us on God's path. It's a journey with many roads. Some of the roads are well traveled, while other paths are yet to be created. But there is only one destination. The few years that we spend on this third planet from the sun are like a vapor in the wind. They are here today and gone tomorrow. Life is short and fleeting; it's a dash. We should live life to the fullest, deriving great joy and happiness from it, and serving and honoring our Heavenly Father every step of the way. He always gives us exactly what we need when we need it, and I'm reminded of that profound truth every time I look at that big furry blessing that is Jag – my trusted confidant, my wise old teacher... my best buddy.

SECTION II

SEE YOU AT THE WAKE

2ND EDITION

HEALING RELATIONSHIPS
BEFORE IT'S TOO LATE

ANTHONY B. LÓPEZ

FOREWORD

No one has to tell you that relationships have a way of breaking down. Every relationship is vulnerable to discord and division. Some seem to be even more fragile than others. The reality is that probably all of us have been part of a broken relationship at some point in our lives. It may have been a relationship that dissolved away on the school playground. Or it may have been one that disintegrated right in your own home. Fortunately for all of us, most of those break-ups wind up being repaired over time. Unfortunately, sometimes they don't.

We probably all know someone who has permanently ended their friendship with another person, or someone who deliberately never communicates with his or her siblings, or someone who rejoices to say that their divorce is final. You may even be that someone.

In a world in which so many material things are made to be disposable when they no longer work, we have somehow found it equally easy to dispose of relationships that aren't working either. I suppose that's simpler than trying to repair them.

The author of this book is convinced that our failure to attempt the repair may be due to the fact that we lack the necessary tools and expertise for the task. So, on the pages to follow he has methodically laid the groundwork for identifying the problem and mapping out the solution.

Of course, you understand that a solution cannot be realized by the mere reading of this book. What you read must be prayerfully and carefully applied. Didn't the wise student of an ever wiser teacher once say that "doing needs to follow hearing," and that "faith without works is dead"?

Assuming that the person you've had a falling out with is still alive, it's not too late to attempt reconciliation. It may never happen if you wait for them to make the first move. But, it could happen if you move first. Are you afraid? Are you feeling unsure? That's understandable. However, if you wait too long you may be too late. You might wind up like one of those who, at funeral homes every day, find themselves filled with regret about what could have been – if only they had tried.

So read this book, friend. Read it with an open heart as well as open eyes. And when you are done reading, reach out and be reconciled!

Pastor D.E. Rabineau
Evangel Chapel
Bridgewater, New Jersey

THE LONG RIDE HOME

The sun was shining brightly. Sam squinted even behind his stylish sunglasses. The thought crossed his mind to close the sunroof but it was such a beautiful warm spring day that he could not bring himself to do it. He glanced over at Bonnie. Her eyes were closed and her head rested peacefully against the headrest. For a moment he saw her as she was when he first met her more than thirty two years earlier, when they were both just barely sixteen. She was as beautiful today as the day he met her – even more so. She had matured gracefully. He took one look in the rearview mirror and there he saw his wife again, except this time it was in the eyes of Kimberly, his daughter. She was almost seventeen and a homecoming queen in the making. She looked just like her mother had when she was a junior in high school.

"Watch the road, dear," Bonnie said without even opening her eyes. She had sensed Sam's glance. He chuckled and shook his head in amazement at his wife's intuitive connection to him and to Kimberly.

The family rode along for awhile without speaking. There had been mostly silence in the car since they had begun their journey that morning. Soon, Sam's mind was back on the same thoughts he'd had all day. He looked out the windshield of his midnight blue luxury sedan and focused for a moment on the car's hood ornament. It reminded him of his success and how fortunate he had been for the past twenty years. He had a beautiful wife, a lovely daughter, and a five thousand square foot home in an affluent neighborhood. He was a respected member of the community and his church. He had established a company that was now one of the most successful businesses in the state. He had money, status, a great family, health, a membership at an exclusive country club, and a loyal golden retriever. He'd made it! But today, he felt like a total loser.

His emotions ran from self pity to anger. He was angry with God. He was angry with himself. He was angry with his brother. Sam wasn't sure if he wanted to yell or cry, or both. He chose neither.

Kimberly broke the loud silence. "How much further, Dad?" she asked from the back seat.

"Not too much more. I think it's the next exit."

They had been on the road since early that morning, stopping only once during the seven hour drive for a quick lunch break.

Bonnie opened her eyes and took in the surroundings. It looked vaguely familiar to her. It had been a long time since they had been in that part of the state.

"How are you doing?" she asked in a whisper.

Sam sighed deeply and clutched the steering wheel tighter.

Bonnie reached out and covered his clenched fist with her dainty hand. No words; only pure love flowing like a warm, comforting current from her hand into his.

Sam slowed the car as he approached the exit ramp. His heart started to race. He glanced in the mirror to check his tie. He could not remember if he had undone the top button. He hadn't.

"You look fine," Bonnie said.

"I have not worn this suit in a while," Sam said. He looked in the mirror again, this time to make eye contact with Kim. She smiled gently.

"You look very nice, dear," he said. "You both do."

"Oh Dad, you always say that," she said, feigning displeasure. Bonnie chuckled.

Sam pulled up to the stop sign at the top of the ramp. Immediately, both he and Bonnie had the same reaction.

"Wow," she said.

"Yeah!" Sam agreed. "Can you believe this?"

Before them and as far as they could see were buildings. There was the entrance of a huge mall directly in front of them. Off to their left was a Home Depot, a gas station, and several fast food places. To their right they saw an ice cream shop, an electronics store, another gas station, and more fast food joints.

"What's up?" Kimberly asked.

"None of this was here the last time we came up this ramp," Bonnie said with wonderment in her voice. "This was all open fields. As far as the eye could see, it was just corn."

"Wow," Bonnie repeated, with a touch of sadness in her voice. "Has it really been that long?"

Sam shook his head. Was this really the town he grew up in? It was practically unrecognizable. The beeping horn of the car behind him told him it was time to move on.

He turned right and traveled two and a half miles in the direction he knew would lead him toward Main Street. On both sides of the road where there had once been open land, there was now was a continuous row of cookie-cutter strip malls and office buildings.

"Incredible," Bonnie muttered, mesmerized.

Finally, Sam recognized something. Coming up on his right was the Methodist Church. It stood proudly, not looking any worse for wear. The church marked the beginning of Main Street coming from the southern end of town. Suddenly he and Bonnie were transported back into the past. Sam slowed the car to a crawl. It was a Saturday afternoon, and he expected that the shops would be open and people would be out and about. He wanted to take it all in slowly. Or maybe he was just afraid to get to their destination.

"Oh look, honey!" Bonnie squealed like a little girl. "Mr. Ruffles Bakery Shop – and there's Mr. Ruffles sweeping his sidewalk."

"Oh, my goodness," Sam replied. "He's had that bakery for more than forty years, and he was always sweeping that front sidewalk in the afternoon."

"Hi, Mr. Ruffles," Bonnie said as she waved behind the car's closed window, fully expecting the man to recognize her.

Mr. Ruffles looked up as though he had heard her and waved back. He waved at everyone. He always wore a smile.

Bonnie's expression turned quickly from excitement to sadness. "He looks so old," she said.

"He must be eighty five years old by now," Sam said. "Well, at least the town hasn't changed much."

"No, it looks just as pretty as when we lived here," Bonnie said.

Both Bonnie and Sam had grown up in Macytown. Main Street was their street. Bonnie's dad had been the town's banker, and she had lived in a beautiful Victorian home just off the main drag. Sam's dad was the owner of the town's deli and had built a home above and behind the store. It was on the north side of Main Street.

Before long, they were driving past the center of the small town. The courthouse looked regal - it had clearly had a facelift.

"Pete's Soda Shop!" Now it was Sam squealing like a little boy.

"A soda shop?" Kimberly said in disbelief. "I thought those only existed in old movies."

"Your dad asked me out for the first time in that soda shop," Bonnie said, smiling. Sam smiled back.

There were some new restaurants on the road, and a few more of the Victorian homes that lined the street had been converted to bed and breakfast inns. A few were in disrepair.

Then Sam came to a red light.

"This wasn't here before," he said. "It used to be a stop sign."

"There's the church your dad and I were married in," Bonnie said to Kimberly as she pointed to the brick and stone building on the corner. The church marquee was a bit fancier than she remembered it, but the service schedule and the name of the Pastor had not changed. Pastor Reed had led that congregation for over forty years. On the front lawn of the church, another sign was posted. It read, "We'll miss you Mike." Sam felt his eyes well up with tears. Bonnie's lip trembled.

"Oh, Sam," she sighed.

The light turned green, and Sam instinctively went one block north and turned right. He knew that's where he would find the funeral home. As he approached, he saw people mingling around the front entrance. He recognized some, but not all. One person immediately pointed at his car and Sam could read his lips. "Hey there's Sam," he said. Sam did his best to return his smile.

"Is that Joe?" Bonnie asked.

"Yeah, that's Joe."

"Who's Joe?" Kimberly asked.

"He was your dad's and Michael's best friend in high school," Bonnie answered. "Oh my, he's completely bald."

Sam pulled into the lot across the street from the funeral home and found a parking spot.

"Well, here we are," he said, mostly to himself.

They all stepped out of the car and before Sam could put on his double breasted black jacket, Joe was there to meet him.

"Sam!" he exclaimed.

"Hi, Joe," Sam said, trying not to let his quivering voice break down.

Joe threw his arms around Sam and hugged him tightly. "It's so good to see you, man," he whispered in Sam's ear.

Sam held on. He was not going to let go first. He could not. Joe put his hand on the back of Sam's head to cradle it onto his shoulder, and Sam broke down and sobbed.

After what seemed like a long time, Joe loosened his grip and smiled at Bonnie. Her face was painted with grief.

"Bonnie, you look incredible. You are as beautiful as ever. I'm still mad at you for marrying this guy instead of me," he said as he gave her a long bear hug.

"It's good to see you too, Joe," she said, running her hand across his cheek.

Joe turned to Kimberly and shook his head.

"Wow, you look just like your mother," he said. "I'm Joe, but you can call me 'Uncle Joe.'" He gave the girl a hug.

"Okay... Uncle Joe," Kim replied, shrugging her shoulders at her mom.

"Who's inside, Joe?" Sam asked.

"Everyone," he answered solemnly.

"Mom?"

"She's here. She's doing okay."

Sam was anxious to see his mother so he could judge her state of mind for himself. For more than two decades she had endured the pain of the bitter feud between her sons, Sam and Mike, and it had been hard on her. Twenty-five years ago, before Sam had left town, their father died and left the deli business to him and Mike. Sam wanted to sell the business, go to college and have a career in law, but Mike wanted them both to stay and run the deli. They couldn't come to an agreement, and it led to a huge fight. Strong words had been said, and fierce blows had been delivered that left wounds that remained open to this day. Yet somehow, they now seemed completely unimportant.

Sam, Bonnie, Kim and Joe walked across the street to the funeral home's entrance. Sam shook a few hands and looked into the eyes of people he had not seen in over twenty years.

When he got inside the funeral home, the first person he saw was Pastor Reed.

"Hello, Sam. It's been a long time," the Pastor said warmly.

"Too long," Sam responded. "It's good to see you, Pastor."

"I've missed you, Sam," the Pastor said, putting an arm around him.

"Where's my mother?" Sam asked.

"Come, I'll take you to her."

Sam followed the pastor to a room full of people.

"Everyone is here for Mike," Pastor Reed said. "He was well loved."

"By everyone except his own brother," Sam whispered.

The pastor stopped and faced Sam.

"You loved your brother, Sam. And he loved you. I know that for a fact. You two stubborn mules just never realized how foolish you both acted over all these years," said the Pastor, with a tinge of anger in his voice. "I can't tell you the number of times we spoke about you two. Sadly, you guys waited just a bit too long. And now here we are, at the wake."

Pastor Reed turned away from Sam. "I've seen more family reunions in this place than any other," he said softly. "'See you at the wake,' I always say to them."

He shook his head and turned back to Sam. "The good news is that it's not too late to salvage relationships with the rest of your family and friends," he said with kindness, placing his hand on Sam's shoulder.

Sam nodded in agreement and then, suddenly, before him stood his mother, tears running freely down her cheeks. Sam melted into her arms, and they both cried.

INTRODUCTION

If we give it some thought, perhaps without much effort, we can each name someone in our immediate family with whom we've had a terrible fight in the past. If you are fortunate enough to be one of the few who has not experienced this, you almost certainly know someone else who has had a major disagreement with a close family member with whom they are now estranged.

It is also likely that we can name someone, perhaps even ourselves, who has not spoken to a close family member in weeks, months, and in some cases, years. How is it I can state this with such confidence? The reason is that since the beginning of time, breakdowns in family relationships have plagued mankind. It is the worst and longest lasting epidemic in the history of human existence. And while other diseases have been eradicated with the advancements in medicine and technology, this steady killer has gone relatively unnoticed and been allowed to perpetuate. It may not be a physiological medical condition, but it is no less debilitating and hazardous to our health than the worst forms of cancer. It has probably claimed more victims than most all other diseases. It has destroyed more lives, broken more spirits, and caused more psychological pain than most wars in history.

It took only four chapters and eight verses of the very first book in the Bible for the first major family breakdown to occur:

Genesis 4:8

Now Cain said to his brother Abel, 'Let's go out to the field,' and while they were in the field, Cain attacked his brother Abel and killed him.

91

The story of one brother hating the other – even to the point of violence – has repeated itself ever since. Fortunately not all family breakdowns end in the loss of life. More often than not what is lost is time. Days, months, and years can go by before brothers will make up with brothers, a sister will talk again to her sister, a mother sees her children, or a father speaks to his sons or daughters.

Sadly, as in the fictional story of Sam and Mike, we sometimes wait too long to make up with those we have fought. We let everything, including our ego, pride, distance, busy lives, and countless other excuses keep us from fixing the broken relationship. It isn't until the death of our family member that we finally break down and cry our hearts out at the wake and beg for forgiveness from a corpse, which is a futile effort, to say the least. How we wish we had not waited so long! Or, we wait until our "enemy" is seriously ill and is knocking at death's door before going to visit with them, and after nearly drowning in a flood of tears, we finally make up. While this is certainly better than waiting until after they are dead we can still never make up for the time apart.

The first edition of *See You at the Wake* was published in 2004 shortly after my mother died of cancer. My mother's strained relationships with her sisters and her father were part of my motivation to write on this subject. For most of her adult life my mom had an estranged relationship with her sisters, especially with Elisa, her youngest sister. Elisa and Mom hardly spoke to each other for more than thirty years. I recall as a teenager visiting my aunt's house only once or twice. I met my cousins then, but the relationships never flowered. The only other times I remember seeing my aunt was when we attended my grandfather's funeral and a few years later when we buried my grandmother.

Many years went by and life went on. Then cancer attacked my mother and life changed for all of us. One evening not long before my mother died, the doorbell rang. When I opened the door, I froze, shocked to find a woman who looked just like my mother had a few years earlier. It was as though I was looking directly into my mother's face. Aunt Elisa stood there elegantly dressed – just like Mom, she was always a stylish and graceful woman. I welcomed her into the home, and after some pleasantries I sat with her and prepared her for the visit with Mom.

I explained to Aunt Elisa that Mom was extremely weak and looked quite frail. I did not want her to be shocked at what she was about to see.

I also asked her to stay as positive as she could. Well, that was pointless. As soon as she entered Mom's room and saw her lying nearly lifeless in the bed, Elisa broke down crying and fell into my mother's arms. Both women were wracked with sobs, crying for all the years they had wasted – all the precious moments together that were now lost forever. I carry the pain of that scene with me to this day. Why had they waited so long?

Mom died shortly after her reunion with Elisa. I wonder how much regret she took to the grave with her. Elisa lives in Florida. I wonder how much regret she's living with now.

In this short book we will explore the reasons why family breakdowns occur and what we can do to prevent them. We will also discover what we can do to fix relationships after they are broken. The Bible, as it does for every other human condition and question, provides us with all the guidance and answers we need. It is my sincere prayer that this book will help you heal relationships with your family and friends, and that it will help you help others do the same.

Let's not wait for the wake.

CHAPTER ONE

Why Family Members Fight

Can you count the stars in a cloudless night sky? How about the trees in a dense forest, or the cars on a Los Angeles freeway during rush hour? You can no more do these things than you can make an exhaustive list of the reasons why family members fight. Each person can compile their own unique and special list that, for one or more of its nuances, would apply to their family and their family alone. Most of us can relate stories of fights, arguments, debates or disputes between members of our immediate or extended families. Often, thank God, these stories have a happy ending, and memories of them are cause for laughter at family reunions when we reminisce about the silliness of The Fight. Sadly however, in other families these memories leave behind deep scars and bruised feelings that over time generate resentment and offer a fertile ground for the seeds of family division to take root and grow.

While it is impossible to list all the reasons why family members fight, perhaps we can succeed in grouping them into categories. Doing so will help us understand the most common origins of discord between family and friends, which will help us be proactive and prevent the breakdowns from occurring in the first place, or at least help us deal with them once they have occurred and move us toward a healing resolution.

Why do family members fight? There are many reasons. Here are just a few:

+ Preferential treatment of one sibling or another by parents
+ One family member cheats another

+ One family member lies to the other
+ One family member steals from another
+ Arguments over how and where to spend the holidays
+ The personal behavior of one sibling displeases or embarrasses the other
+ Financial (and social status) differences between siblings or family members
+ Disputes over inheritance or insurance benefits left behind by a family member
+ Medical conditions of a member or members of the family (caretaking responsibilities)
+ Disliking the spouse of a family member
+ Lack of respect for each other
+ Attitude or perceived arrogance of one family member by another

Before we analyze these points individually, please note that while this list speaks of siblings and family members, one can replace the words "sibling" or "family member" with the word "friend" and the same statements would apply in most cases. For instance, friendships may break down if one friend lies to the other, or if they cheat each other, or if they argue over respect, behavior, or attitudes. We will primarily focus on relationships between family members and siblings throughout the text, but clearly the concepts, ideas, and lessons apply to our relationships with friends as well.

Now let's look at each of the common reasons for family discord.

Preferential treatment

<u>Genesis 37:3-4</u>

Now [Jacob] <u>loved Joseph more</u> than any of his <u>other sons,</u> <u>because</u> he had been born to him in his old age; and <u>he made</u> <u>a richly ornamented robe for him</u>. When his <u>brothers saw</u> that their father loved him more than any of them, <u>they hated</u> <u>him</u> and could <u>not speak</u> a kind word to him."

This passage of scripture is one of the clearest examples of a parent exhibiting preferential treatment of one sibling over another. There are many other such examples in the Bible. But in these two verses we gain valuable insight into how it can happen, how it is manifested, and what the end result can be when a parent does this. The key ideas in the verse are underlined. Let's consider these points:

a. "...[Jacob] loved Joseph more..." Human nature may make it very difficult for a parent not to be more partial to one child than another. It can be intentional or completely innocent. More than likely, the latter is the case. Nevertheless, the impact of such behaviors and attitudes will undoubtedly have an impact on all children involved.

The word "because" introduces the reasons why Jacob loved Joseph more than the others. Parents may treat one child differently (and better) than the others for an infinite number of reasons. It could be because one child has a greater athletic ability than the others, or maybe because one can sing better than the others. The reasons can be as varied as the personalities of the children. They can include:

+ the children's temperaments
+ their attitudes
+ their appearances
+ their behaviors
+ their intelligence levels
+ how obedient they are
+ how well they do in school
+ their similarity to the parent
+ how popular they are with their friends, and
+ whether they are male or female

The reasons can go on and on. Parents, whether consciously or subconsciously, tend to pick favorites with their children. Is that so bad? Can it be avoided? Can parents do something about it? Can this affect the long term relationship between family members and be a major contributing cause to severing ties with some? The answers to these questions are yes, yes, yes, and yes!

Is it so bad for a parent to pick favorites? Parents must never underestimate the awesome power that they possess to influence their children's thinking, attitude, self image, and development. Eleanor Roosevelt once said, "No one can make you feel inferior without your consent." I think she was almost 100% correct, but I would add the words "except your parents" to the end of her statement. As parents, our words and our behaviors can either build our children up or tear them down. We can either help them establish healthy relationships with their siblings, or create opportunities for division.

Can these preferences be avoided? Of course they can. Parents must simply take responsibility for loving all of their children unconditionally and equally. Period. No excuses. The consequences of not doing so are too great to wonder or debate whether or not it's okay.

Next, can parents do something about it? The answer again is yes. Parents must labor to love their children equally, while maybe not in the same way. We must understand and adjust to our children's personalities and styles and love them in ways that make sense to them! We must discover them and fully develop the best qualities in our children and teach them to deal with those areas in which they do not excel. Moreover, we must always carefully consider our words and actions and the messages they send to all the children. Jacob's gift of a special coat to his son Joseph was a clear indication to the other brothers and sisters that Joseph was the preferred one.

b. "When his brothers saw…" Parental behaviors are visible to everyone in the family. Whether it is a word, a gift, or simply an attitude toward one child or another, there will be no secrecy about the message. Sooner or later it will be clear to all. Joseph's brothers already knew that he was Jacob's favorite; the coat was simply a visible reminder to them.

c. "…they hated him…" This outcome is what my daughter Cristina would call a "duh." You know that response don't you? It's the one when you get that weird dumb look on your face. Could Jacob expect any outcome other than the one he got? Could he have expected the other children to love the fact that Joseph was getting special treatment over them? Joseph's brothers hated him! This was the direct result of their father's behavior. How many brothers and sisters have hidden – and not so hidden – ill feelings toward each other because of the way their parents treated them? It is rare to find a set of siblings that, when pressed, will not admit that they felt that Mom or Dad treated their sister or brother better than they were treated.

d. "...could not speak a kind word..." Once feelings of dislike or hatred are in the mix of the family dynamics, it often leads to a communications shutdown. That may not mean that siblings don't talk with one another. It may, however, mean that communications become shallow and casual rather than deep and intimate the way communications between people who love each other should be.

Preferential treatment of one sibling over another by a parent can be the root cause of a family dispute that lasts an entire lifetime. Parents must not allow themselves to be the source of such ill feelings. If you are a parent, make sure you are not behaving in this way toward your children. If you are the child of a parent who played favorites, know that it can get in the way of a healthy relationship with your brother or sister only if you allow it to! Neither your brother nor your sister is to blame for the turmoil caused by your parents' conduct. However, now it's up to you. We each have the choice of letting it remain a problem or going beyond the hurt feelings and enjoying a healthy and fun relationship with our siblings. Choose wisely. Choose joy!

A family member cheats another

Genesis 27:41

Esau held a grudge against Jacob because of the blessing his father had given him.

Genesis 27:35-36:

But he said, "Your brother came deceitfully and took your blessing." Esau said, "Isn't he rightly named Jacob? He has deceived me these two times: He took my birthright and now he's taken my blessing!"

There is probably no worse feeling in the world than being cheated. It is no different than if you came home and found your apartment ransacked by thieves with no regard for your privacy. You feel violated! The feeling you get when someone cheats you is even more painful when the cheater is someone you love and trust. No doubt this is why a spouse is so deeply hurt when their soul mate commits adultery.

The story of Jacob and Esau has all the elements of a long term family dispute. By today's television standards, it would make the plot of a soap opera that could successfully run for years. It has: brother cheating brother, brother cheating father, mother helping brother cheat the father, parent showing preferential treatment of one sibling over another, and brother wanting to kill brother. And this is just where the story begins! Act Two features mother helping brother escape the wrath of the other brother by sending him to live with the not-so-honest uncle. This uncle tricks the brother into marrying his oldest daughter, forcing him to work seven additional years to marry the woman he really loves.

Years go by, and both brothers prosper and have great wealth, but don't see each other for many years. In the meantime, there are marriages, births of children, deaths of friends, happy moments, sad moments, and angry moments. Life goes on. One day one brother decides that he wants to get back together with his brother, so he sends bribes to his brother to try to ease his anger. Eventually, the two brothers get back together and there is a happy family reunion. Sounds just like the soap opera *All My Children*, doesn't it? Sadly, this story is repeated over and over again in many families, except that it's not a television show, it's for real.

Often, a sibling can hold a grudge for years, never really talking about it but certainly acting on it. Whether we like it or not we behave in ways consistent with our inner feelings. Therefore, if we feel angry toward someone, we may have a short temper with them, or we may find ways to criticize and verbally hurt the person with whom we are angry. Sometimes we may have a subtle arrogance toward the person who cheated us. Our true feelings are demonstrated either in small incremental ways or in blowout arguments. One thing is always certain: true feelings will come out somehow, and the signals sent and received are crystal clear.

Both the sender and the receiver have a perfect understanding of their meaning and impact. Sadly, neither the sender nor the receiver may truly understand *why* it's happening.

One way this is evident is: when The Fight finally does take place, it is then – perhaps for the first time – that the person who has been feeling cheated tries to verbalize what they feel. This raw, spontaneous emotion comes spewing out and it is not well articulated or measured. Is that any real surprise? Think back to a time when you were angry and exchanged harsh words with someone. Did you later wish you could take back some of the things you said? Almost everyone can think of such a time. Some of us don't have to think past the last few minutes!

Trying to have a rational discussion with someone when you are angry is nearly impossible. In the middle of an argument, the person trying to explain their anger over being cheated can end up sounding like a nitpicker who is making more of the incident than they should. That is, they may bring up something that happened many years earlier – even from their childhood. Can you picture someone saying, "You always have to have what I have; like the time you asked Sally out for a date when you knew I liked her!" Sounds silly? You don't think it happens? Many of you reading this can think of many silly things said in the heat of a fight. To the person saying it, this may have been a traumatic and significant episode which left them feeling resentful and vengeful for years. To the other sibling it may have been an insignificant teenage spat that took place thirty years earlier – one that he had completely forgotten about. Sometimes the stories are exaggerated and or the facts are jumbled, so the accused person becomes defensive and shoots back with issues of his or her own. And so the mudslinging begins. There is one thing that you can always count on when you get into a mud fight: you're going to get dirty!

What should we do? Well, if we feel cheated, speak up about it! Don't wait until all the pent up anger decides to erupt like an uncontrolled volcano. And if you are at the receiving end and are accused of having cheated in some way, try your best to listen without becoming defensive and without minimizing your loved ones feelings. For both parties involved – whether you are the victim or the accused cheater – there is one rule that must never be violated: never try to discuss the issue when emotions are running high and people are angry. Nothing can be solved from a position of anger.

One family member lies to another

Exodus 20:16

You shall not give false testimony against your neighbor.

Lying generates the same feelings as cheating. In fact, lying is just a form of cheating. People lie to improve their position, cover their tracks, take advantage of a situation, create a new reality, fool someone, hide something they are ashamed or afraid of, or simply because it's sometimes easier than dealing with the truth. No matter the reason, lying to someone generates no warm feelings and creates a perfect foundation for a broken relationship. If you've lied to someone, come clean. If someone has lied to you, make him or her come clean. If you wait until The Fight, it may be too late to repair the damage and keep the relationship from breaking down.

A family member steals from another

Exodus 20:15

You shall not steal.

That's the kind of verse that I can just picture God saying: "Any questions?" or "What part of 'You shall not steal' did you not understand?" Yet how common is this among family members? More importantly, how does the one from whom something has been stolen feel? They feel the way Esau did toward Jacob:

Genesis 27:41

Esau held a grudge against Jacob because of the blessing his father had given him. He said to himself, "The days of mourning for my father are near; then I will kill my brother Jacob."

Isn't this a bit extreme? Perhaps. I mean after all, how many guys really mean it when they say they are going to kill their brother? Fortunately, not many! However, we can't ignore the underlying feelings that make someone so angry that they would want someone else dead, or at the very least, to go away. It is these same feelings that make a separation easier to deal with later.

So, if you've cheated your brother or sister, make it right. If something has been stolen from you, as hard as it may be, you must sit down with your brother or sister and have a rational discussion about it. Later on in the text, we will discuss just how to do this.

Arguments over the holidays

The number of family fights that happen each year over where the holidays are going to be celebrated is mindboggling. Holidays are intended to bring families together in celebration of a special occasion. Some of my personal favorites are Thanksgiving, Christmas and New Years Eve. It is on these days, perhaps more than any others, that we should count our blessings, be happy to be together, enjoy each other's company, and munch on some great home cooked meals. Instead, they can become the most stressful days of the year! The tension over who is traveling where, who's coming, and what or whom they are bringing with them can make us crazy. We fight over whether the party should be in our home or at our sister's house.

It's at times like these that people say things like: "why do we always have to have Thanksgiving dinner at your family's house?" and "why can't we travel to my mother's house instead?" Or one brother may say to another, "you always put your wife's side of the family before your own." I admit that this has been an issue in my own family, and I have probably even contributed to it. If I have, I deeply regret it.

It is during these holidays and on other special days throughout the year when the family disputes either tend to begin or come to a head. The arguments escalate to full blown fights, and in some sad cases end in domestic violence. Why is that? The reasons are many, but no doubt a few major contributing factors are:

1. This is one of those times when families come together for a significant amount of time. We first talk about all the superficial

things such as: "How's the job?" or "When did you change your hair style?" or "How did you lose so much weight?" or "Are you dating anyone?" or "How do you like your new car?" After exhausting all the small talk, we are left with an awkward silence. This is usually followed by a bit of television watching, until someone suggests that everyone play a board game. Out comes the Monopoly or Trivial Pursuit, and all happily engage in this fun activity. But somehow, without notice, something happens to cause one person to become upset. Before it can be stopped, an argument ensues that has nothing to do with the game but is rather firmly entrenched in feelings and events from long ago. The argument may sound something like this:

"I'm not playing this stupid game anymore. You are such a cheater. You have not changed a bit from when you were twelve!"

"Me? You mean *you* haven't changed since you were twelve. You still can't accept that I am better than you and I will always win no matter what we're doing."

"You win by cheating. You were always a cheater and a liar. That much will never change."

No doubt, we can each supply our own personal ending to this story. One thing is certain – it can lead nowhere good.

2. Often these gatherings include drinking alcohol as part of the ritual of celebrations. Too much booze leads to loose tongues; loose tongues inevitably lead to dumb things being said; and dumb things being said almost always lead to a fight.

   Psalm 39:1

   I said, "I will watch my ways and keep my tongue from sin; I will put a muzzle on my mouth as long as the wicked are in my presence."

   Psalm 34:13

   ...keep your tongue from evil and your lips from speaking lies.

<u>Psalm 52:2-4</u>

Your tongue plots destruction; it is like a sharpened razor, you who practice deceit. You love evil rather than good, falsehood rather than speaking the truth. You love every harmful word, O you deceitful tongue!

Firearm experts say you should never point a gun at someone unless you intend to shoot them. Our tongues are far more lethal than that! They are like grenades. We should keep them well guarded and with a pin in them, lest they explode in our mouths.

Personal Behavior Differences

It always amazes me how different brothers and sisters can be considering that they come from the same gene pool and that they are usually raised in the same environment. They attend the same schools, go to the same church, are disciplined by the same parents, and even play on the same teams together. Yet from very early on, even as mere infants, parents can tell that their children have completely different temperaments, thought processes, tendencies, and preferences. As the children grow, these differences can – and usually do – become even more accentuated.

Where one sibling may be the consummate athlete, the other may hate sports. While one brother may become a conservative Republican, the other may be as liberal as one can be. Why does this happen? A wide range of theories attempt to explain these fascinating variations among family members, but for the purposes of our discussion we need only acknowledge that variations exist. We can agree that they affect the way people think, the way they feel, and ultimately, the way they behave. These differences are also an excellent source of conflict between family members. And so in relationships in which children have not been taught how to deal with – and indeed, how to celebrate – differences, then these dissimilarities often lead to conflicts and arguments.

These differences not only create conflict between the family members involved, they also generate tension between other immediate and extended family members like parents, cousins, wives, husbands, and even friends, as these seemingly innocent bystanders are forced to choose sides with one sibling or another. They may not even do so consciously, yet by their attitudes and behaviors they migrate closer to the one sibling they tend to favor. The Bible provides a clear example of this phenomenon in the story of Isaac and Rebekah. Isaac favored Esau while Rebekah favored Jacob.

Differences between siblings and family members are not unusual. In fact, they are the norm. The sooner we each realize that it is possible to accept, and even enjoy our differences and learn to love one another unconditionally, the sooner our broken relationships can begin the healing process.

Financial Differences Between Family Members

Search deep – and in some cases not so deep – and you will often find a financial issue as the major contributing factor in a family dispute. Whether it is an attitude about how to spend money or an attitude about having or not having money, family members often measure one another by the size of their bank accounts. Manifested in ways that are usually visible – the size of a house, the type of car, or the clothes worn – financial differences between family members are often blatantly obvious. This can be a huge source of resentment and tension. Rather than rejoicing in a family member's financial success, some grow to dislike it. Clearly, the behavior of the person with the most money can either add to the tension or help reduce it, but as is usually the case, it takes two to tango.

Often, the family member with less financial resources behaves in a way that creates the problem. They may feel somehow cheated because their sibling or family member enjoys a level of success that they do not. They may even think that they have a right to share in the other's wealth. That is, the family member with more should simply give them part of what they have amassed. While it would be nice if the family member with more money decided to spread the wealth around, they surely have no obligation to do so.

If there is a broken relationship in your life and money is at the center of the issue, consider this: If you are the one with the money, look back at your behavior. Carefully examine your attitude. Are you possibly fueling the fire that burned down the bridge between you and another family member? Conversely, if you are the one with less money, are you certain that it's not your jealousy that has caused the rift between you and someone you love? Have you harbored ill will toward someone because they have and you don't? Whatever the case, there is only one thing for you to do: Stop it! Imagine standing before God and hearing him ask, "Are you trying to tell me that you allowed a relationship to break down because of a financial difference between you and your brother?"

What will your honest answer be?

Inheritance or Insurance Disputes

Is there anything sadder than a family embroiled in a bitter legal fight over the inheritance or insurance money left behind in someone's estate? How many families do you suppose have broken up after a deceased grandparent left a few dollars behind for the grandkids to fight over? Once again, picture yourself standing before the Lord and explaining this one!

In my family, my parents will be the first generation to leave any significant estate behind when they go home to be with the Lord. In previous generations, our family was poor and left only a few personal belongings to be divided among their loved ones. In the case of my grandmother on my father's side, she left only a small house on a tiny piece of land in the town of Yauco, Puerto Rico. After the home was sold and the proceeds divided between the numerous brothers and sisters – not to mention the government – the remaining funds were certainly not worth fighting over.

I wonder what would have happened if my grandmother had left an estate worth hundreds of thousands or millions of dollars? Would there have been a peaceful, uncomplicated transaction between brothers and sisters? Or would a wave of cousins, uncles, aunts and other far flung and rarely seen relatives suddenly emerge to claim their fair share of Grandma's Pot of Gold? Would some have argued that the pot's contents were not being divided fairly; that some deserve more than others because they took care of Grandma while everybody else visited once a year on Mother's Day? What if someone claimed that she could prove that Grandma promised her the house, or the land, or the fine jewelry? Perhaps, some would argue, the siblings who were better off financially did not need to get any of the inheritance money? Sadly it does not take much to launch these kinds of intense and often prolonged battles. The only real winners are the attorneys hired to litigate the case.

Some of us could never imagine engaging in a fight over an inheritance. I just can't picture my brother and I in a brawl over who gets what if dad leaves something when he goes to heaven. Frankly, I can't imagine that he feels any differently than I do. Whatever Dad leaves for my brother and me to share, I am certain we will do so happily and with complete respect for our parents' memory. Regrettably, not everyone feels or acts the same way. Dealing with how to divide an estate is often the root of a major family dispute.

Medical Conditions

<u>Mark 2: 3-5:</u>

Some men came, bringing to Him a paralytic, carried by four of them. Since they could not get him to Jesus because of the crowd, they made an opening in the roof above Jesus, and after digging through it, lowered the mat the paralyzed man was lying on. When Jesus saw their faith, He said to the paralytic, "Son, your sins are forgiven."

Dealing with a loved one's medical condition can put a strain on family relationships. Think of the amount of effort that these four men had to go through to get their paralyzed friend to Jesus for healing. It was not a trivial feat. Now consider the effort that it would take to care for a person like this day in and day out for a lifetime! Suppose one sibling is diagnosed or born with a condition that requires constant medical and personal attention. What if this condition renders the person incapable of caring for themselves even in the basic functions of every-day life? Consider for a moment the burden placed on a parent and other family members as it affects their lives over a prolonged period of time; perhaps even over a lifetime. When someone refuses to carry their fair share of the load of caring for the disabled family member either financially or with hands-on involvement, resentment and anger build in those who are picking up the slack. This emotion is often bottled up until suddenly it explodes without warning one day, causing severe damage to the already strained relationship.

Dislike of a family member's spouse or friends

Proverbs 19:13

A foolish son is his father's ruin…

Proverbs 27: 15-16

A quarrelsome wife is like a constant dripping on a rainy day; restraining her is like restraining the wind or grasping oil with the hand.

Genesis 26: 34-35

When Esau was forty years old, he married Judith, daughter of Beeri the Hittite, and also Basemath, daughter of Elon the Hittite. They were a source of grief to Isaac and Rebekah.

How many mother-in-law jokes have you heard? How many of them do you think are close to true? All joking aside, many people look at a family member's choice of spouse and wonder, "What was she smoking when she chose *this* guy?" As a father of two daughters, I know that the standards I have in mind for their future mates are quite likely a bit high. Clark Kent may have a chance of winning my approval, but only if he stops hiding behind those silly glasses and wearing tight jumpsuits. Nevertheless, I hope that I resist the temptation to order a complete FBI background check on the boys who will be calling on my girls. After all, I do want to know of their intentions, their Christian faith, their future educational aspirations and their ability to take care of my princesses financially. Every father wants to know these things! The smarter ones (and I pray that I fall in this group) choose restraint and learn to warm up to their daughter's choice of mate. But fathers don't have a monopoly on this behavior. How many mothers out there have that deep down feeling that a particular girl is not good enough for her little boy – especially when she can't even cook him a good meal!

These are simple and silly examples of how a spouse can cause rifts in a family. But there are many more significant examples in which the spouse – either because of their attitude, behavior, religious belief, race, financial status, educational level, or even their personality – simply rubs other members of the family the wrong way.

We can all think of a person whose choice of a significant other caused family members to distance themselves so much that weeks, months, and even years went by with little or no contact between them. The selection of spouses is extremely important to the long term health of families. However, it is up to each of us to make sure that once the person is in the family, they're in! We must learn to deal with them, love them, and get along with them.

In this chapter we have dealt with just a few examples of why family feuds take place. There are many more. Ultimately, the "why" may not be as important as the "how," the "when," or the "how to fix it." Let's explore those concepts next.

CHAPTER TWO

Reasons and Excuses

Even in relationships that are sound and healthy, finding time to be with family members can be a challenge. When there is a strained relationship, or worse yet, one that is broken, making the time to be with one another becomes a challenge of herculean proportions. Understanding the problem is part of the solution. So, let's consider a few of the reasons why family members don't see each other and what we should do about it.

Busy Lives and Priorities

Psalm 46:10

Be still and know that I am God; I will be exalted among the nations, I will be exalted in the earth.

I live by "to do" lists. All Type-A personalities probably do. If it's got to get done, it gets put on a list with a priority. The problem with the list is that it never gets shorter. There is always something being added to the list. Some people have honey-do lists. That's when your spouse says, "Honey, do this," or "Honey, do that." Honey-do lists never get shorter either – take it from a guy who knows. The Internet and e-mail may be the single greatest invention in the 20th Century. It may also hold the distinct honor of being the greatest time thief. Between checking e-mails, voice mail, regular mail, and junk mail, we barely have time to do anything else.

For some people, business travel can also be a consideration. It certainly is for me! Whether I am up and down all day long in a car or getting on an airplane and flying across the nation for meetings, travel saps my energy and time. Then of course there are church activities. All of this is followed by the kid's soccer, tennis, football, basketball, and karate. Once in a while you find some quiet time to read and play the piano, but not much.

When you consider the amount of time you spend at work, in traffic, getting the kids to and from church and school activities, cleaning the house, cooking the meals, doing the laundry, grooming the dog and preparing for the next day, it's amazing we even have time to sleep. That's life today; fast food, fast cars, and fast computers. "I just called to say a quick hello!" is our message on the answering machine of someone we actually wanted to talk to. Who then would have time to try to talk to someone we happen to be fighting with? "I'll think about that tomorrow". "Why add more stress to my life now?" "I don't have time to deal with his silliness right now." These are our thoughts as we quickly dismiss the idea of calling someone with whom we are feuding.

We lead very busy lives. Yet God exalts us to be still and know that He is God. How I wish I could do that more! The Bible tells us there is a time for everything:

Ecclesiastes 3:1-8

> *There is a time for everything, and a season for every activity under heaven: a time to be born and a time to die, a time to plant and a time to uproot, a time to kill and a time to heal, a time to tear down and a time to build, a time to weep and a time to laugh, a time to mourn and a time to dance, a time to scatter stones and a time to gather them, a time to embrace and a time to refrain, a time to search and a time to give up, a time to keep and a time to throw away, a time to tear and a time to mend, a time to be silent and a time to speak, a time to love and a time to hate, a time for war and a time for peace.*

What powerful lessons are found in this passage! There is indeed a time for everything, and God planned it that way. That includes time to heal, time to embrace, time to speak, and time to love! We must make time in our lives for these things or we miss out on God's perfect plan for our lives.

Somebody once said, "If the devil can't make you sin, he'll make you busy." There is much truth in that statement. As long as you don't have time to do something about your broken relationships, nothing will happen with your broken relationships. If fixing them is not a priority, if it's not on the top of your to-do list, forget about it! It simply will not happen.

One last thought on busy lives:

Luke 10: 38–42

> *As Jesus and his disciples were on their way, he came to a village where a woman named Martha opened her home to him. She had a sister called Mary, who sat at the Lord's feet listening to what he said. But Martha was distracted by all the preparations that had to be made. She came to him and asked, "Lord, don't you care that my sister has left me to do the work by myself? Tell her to help me!" "Martha, Martha," the Lord answered, "you are worried and upset about many things, but only one thing is needed. Mary has chosen what is better, and it will not be taken away from her."*

Mary chose wisely. Martha worried fruitlessly. Choose wisely. Put first things first and make sure that your priorities are in the right order. Fixing your relationships with family members must be at the top of the list of things to do. You should have a sense of urgency about this. Something unimportant will always get in your way if you let it. You will always be able to find some excuse not to deal with your broken relationships. None of them are valid! Time is running out. Don't wait any longer to reach out to the one you love.

Distance between each other

We live in a society and at a time when many family members are separated by neighborhoods, cities, states, and even countries. Long gone are the days when families all lived in the same neighborhood and in many cases in the same house. Now, careers, schools, lifestyles and other things determine where people end up setting roots. In many more cases, families are nomadic, moving every couple of years chasing career opportunities or simply escaping to the other side of the fence.

We all know that the grass is always greener on the other side of the fence. What we don't seem to realize is that sometimes that grass is greener because it is fertilized. It is fertilized with hard work, loving relationships, and a healthy balance between work and family. Perhaps we should consider fertilizing our own grass rather than seeking to jump the fence. Nevertheless the reasons for families to have great physical distance between them are many.

In my case, I have family living in more than ten states and fifteen cities. Some even live across an ocean in Puerto Rico. Even with the advent of the internet, e-mail, voice mail, cellular phones and every other sophisticated piece of satellite communication hardware available today, bridging the gap between family members is hard. We may see each other at family reunions, Thanksgiving, Christmas, Easter or a few other special holidays. We may speak on the phone once in a while, but we never write letters anymore. Who has time?

So what should we do about this? What else? Try harder! Put staying in touch with your family members on your to-do list. Tell someone in your immediate family or a good friend to hold you accountable for staying in touch with them. Have someone ask you regularly if you've written to your sister, called your dad, or scheduled that visit to your brother's house. This takes work. Hard work! But when all is said and done, it's some of the most rewarding work you'll ever do.

Fear of being hurt

The story of how Jacob and Esau dealt with their broken relationship is especially profound. In this story we can see everything that caused the breakdown in the first place to how it is ultimately resolved. From the moment of their twin birth, we see a dynamic between these two brothers that became fertile ground for the deception that Jacob eventually perpetrated on Esau. Jacob had ambition, smarts, and a special place in his mother's heart. But what he did not have was the birthright of a firstborn son. That belonged to Esau. From a very young age, Jacob – at times even with the help of his mother – did everything possible to take this birthright from his brother. He eventually succeeded in stealing it by fooling their father. This led to a complete breakdown of their relationship and to Jacob fleeing from his homeland to escape his brother's wrath. It would be years before the two would ever see each other again. Eventually, after many years, Jacob decides that it is time to reunite with his brother.

Genesis 32:3-9

Jacob sent messengers ahead of him to his brother Esau in the land of Seir, the country of Edom. He instructed them: "This is what you are to say to my master Esau: 'Your servant Jacob says, I have been staying with Laban and have remained there till now. I have cattle and donkeys, sheep and goats, menservants and maidservants. Now I am sending this message to my lord, that I may find favor in your eyes.'" "When the messengers returned to Jacob, they said, "We went to your brother Esau, and now he is coming to meet you, and four hundred men are with him." In great fear and distress Jacob divided the people who were with him into two groups, and the flocks and herds and camels as well. He thought, "If Esau comes and attacks one group, the group that is left may escape." Then Jacob prayed, "O God of my father Abraham, God of my father Isaac, O LORD, who said to me, 'Go back to your country and your relatives, and I will make you prosper,'

Now, there's a guy that is worried about meeting his estranged brother! He sends word ahead of his arrival, and refers to Esau as his lord and to himself as Esau's servant. He also makes sure that he sends a healthy bribe. Oxen, donkeys, and even servants are what Jacob is hoping will buy down his brother's anger. It is interesting to note that Jacob assumes that Esau must still be angry with him, even though he has not seen his brother in many years. We can only guess at why he believed that. One possible reason is that he put himself in his brother's shoes and realized that he likely would still be angry and unable to forgive his brother if the situation were reversed.

Not only was Jacob afraid, but when he learned that Esau was on his way to meet him accompanied by four hundred men, he must have felt his heart sink down to his feet. We might have the same sinking feeling when we consider making that first contact with an estranged family member. Our mind races as it considers all the possible negative outcomes that could result from our pending encounter. No doubt some people fear for their safety, as did Jacob. Sadly, domestic violence is common in our world today, and family disputes sometimes do end in bloodshed.

However, like Jacob, we must not be deterred by this fear. Jacob was fearful of Esau but he was determined to reunite with his brother. So he prepared for the event. First, he sent advance messages to try to smooth the way. What can we do in advance of our reunion to smooth the way? Perhaps we can write a letter to the person we are fighting with, or make a phone call first. No doubt, we should pray to prepare. What else can we do to pave the way to healing? Short of sending a bribe like Jacob did, might there be some other olive branch that we can extend to the person with whom we are fighting?

Next, we should follow Jacob's example and prepare a contingency plan.

<u>Genesis 32:7-8</u>

In great fear and distress Jacob divided the people who were with him into two groups, and the flocks and herds and camels as well. ⁸ *He thought, "If Esau comes and attacks one group, the group that is left may escape."*

<u>Genesis 32:11-18</u>

"Save me, I pray, from the hand of my brother Esau, for I am afraid he will come and attack me, and also the mothers with their children. But you have said, 'I will surely make you prosper and will make your descendants like the sand of the sea, which cannot be counted.'" He spent the night there, and from what he had with him he selected a gift for his brother Esau: two hundred female goats and twenty male goats, two hundred ewes and twenty rams, thirty female camels with their young, forty cows and ten bulls, and twenty female donkeys and ten male donkeys. He put them in the care of

his servants, each herd by itself, and said to his servants, "Go ahead of me, and keep some space between the herds." He instructed the one in the lead: "When my brother Esau meets you and asks, 'To whom do you belong, and where are you going, and who owns all these animals in front of you?' then you are to say, 'They belong to your servant Jacob. They are a gift sent to my lord Esau, and he is coming behind us.' "

Jacob had a plan. First, he prayed to God and asked for intervention. Smart man! Why not try this on your own? Tap into the power of The Almighty. Next, Jacob continued to humble himself before his brother by sending gifts, and referring to Esau as lord and to himself as servant. If we want to heal relationships, we ought not to have an arrogant attitude about the healing process. Jacob was wise enough to know that a humble spirit is always a great place to start.

Have you prayed about the relationship you want to heal? Have you made a plan of reconciliation? Is your heart in the right place? Are you humble or arrogant? Have you forgiven your family member even before they ask? Start today.

Fear of rejection

One day when Marisa was seven years old, she was moping around the house. When I asked her what was wrong, she said she was bored. It was a cold winter afternoon and she really did not want to go outside to play. So I said to her, "Why don't you call Amanda and see if she can come over and play with you a while?" Her response was interesting.

"I'm afraid to," she said.

"Afraid of what?" I asked.

"She might say no," Marisa replied.

"You won't know until you ask," I explained.

Then Marisa confessed, "Yeah, but I don't want to take that chance."

It's amazing how a seven year old understands the concept of rejection! Marisa was concerned about getting turned down. The fear almost kept her from calling. But when she finally got the courage to call, it turned out better than she expected. She ended up getting invited to Amanda's house and had a wonderful play date.

Don't allow fear of rejection to paralyze you. Is there a chance that you will be rejected as you try to reach out to someone who is not yet ready to communicate with you? Yes. So what? Keep trying. Are you going to let a bit of rejection – which is nothing more than an attack on your ego – keep you from salvaging a lifelong family relationship? Try explaining that one to a seven year old!

Different religious or political beliefs

Few philosophical differences are more difficult to bridge than religious or political beliefs. Embedded in these beliefs are the fundamental tenets that define most people – the principles by which we choose to live our lives. These beliefs define who and what we are. They dictate what we support, and can restrict our ability to understand different points of views or accept a different way of doing things. They provide us with group memberships that offer us status and a sense of belonging.

A person who lives according to the Jewish religion could no more accept Christ as the Son of God and Savior than a Christian would be willing to abandon that belief. This one point of difference has been the cause of human conflict since Jesus walked on this Earth. A Republican thinks taxes should be lowered while a Democrat wants bigger government. A pro-life person believes that aborting a baby is morally wrong and should never be an option, while a pro-abortion person sees that same baby as a woman's choice. One person believes in capital punishment and in the principles of "an eye for an eye;" the other believes that killing by the state is just that – killing. The Catholic person believes Mary remained a virgin her entire life, while the Protestant believes Mary had other children after the virgin birth of Jesus. One person believes that interracial marriages are okay while others are violently opposed to them.

These differences are not unusual among friends and coworkers, but they're also not unusual among the closest of blood relatives. Many family disputes and separations are founded in religious and political differences. A son from a white family marries an African-American woman and suddenly he's an outcast. A daughter abandons Judaism, accepts Jesus Christ as her Savior and marries a Baptist man, and her father wants nothing more to do with her. An American-born man abandons his country and its ideals and joins the Taliban – sworn enemies of the United States and its citizens. And so on and so on.

We've probably all had lively discussions with family, friends, coworkers and sometimes even strangers on the issues of politics, religion, education and sports. How often have these discussions led to heated debates and escalated into all out shouting matches? In my family, it's one of our favorite pastimes! My dad, brother, and I just love to "argue" over political issues, investment strategies, and anything else that comes up when we are together. An outside observer might think that we are having a brawl, but we are not. Oh, I admit there have been occasions when we had huge family arguments. But most of our debates are not serious fights. In fact, sometimes one of us will argue a position we don't even agree with, just to keep a debate alive! It is always fairly easy to tell the real fights from the fun ones.

Here are the important things to remember about religious and political differences and their impact on family relationships:

1. They exist. The differences are there, and to some extent they define who we are and how we behave. So being aware of them is of paramount importance if we are going to effectively deal with them.

2. We must be sensitive to our loved ones' points of view. This does not mean you have to agree with them or support their views and ideals. For instance, your brother may believe that abortion is okay. It's not. He would be wrong. But to continuously fight over that issue would be pointless and bear nothing but sour fruit. Does that mean that you never discuss the issue with him? The answer is no. However, knowing his position will help you better prepare to have productive discussions with him. Listen to his position. Understand his position. The best way to debate someone is to know exactly what their position is! Then, being careful not to attack your brother, deal with the issue. Voice your disagreement with his opinion, but not with him personally. Present your views and positions in a nonthreatening way. Ask to be heard. Fighting over these important issues is never productive. Debating and fighting are two very different things.

3. Set rules for discussions on issues that you know can be volatile. If your sister is a diehard conservative Republican and you have

liberal views, you are bound to have disagreements. But the one thing you can agree to is what the rules of engagement will be for your debates. Remember: you are sisters first and political entities second.

4. Know when to back off. You don't always have to win! Sometimes, we try too hard to convince someone that we are right and they are wrong that all we truly accomplish is starting a huge fight and increasing the separation between us. A Christian who wants nothing more than seeing all his family members become born-again believers can be as persistent as a hungry dog chewing on a bone. There is probably nothing more important than having those we love come to the saving knowledge of Jesus Christ! But how many stories have you heard from non-Christians who say that their brother is a religious nut? Or that their sister is in some kind of cult and wants them to join; or that they avoid calling their mother because all she ever wants to talk about is Jesus. How about the husband who was born again after twenty years of marriage, and suddenly becomes a religious freak and wants his wife to do the same? We can turn people away and create greater distance between us if we try to force our beliefs – whether they're political or religious – on our family members. This does not mean we don't try; it just means we are smart about how we go about it.

Differences in economic standing

Nothing creates barriers between people faster than money. In the world in which we live, the thickness of your wallet often determines how you are treated.

If you have financial wealth, consider yourself blessed! But know that your wealth can be a barrier to family members who have less. Don't flaunt your wealth; it will do that all by itself.

If you don't have financial wealth, consider yourself blessed! But know that your lack of wealth can be a barrier for family members who have more.

Money – or the lack of it – puts us in different socio-economic circles. Having money creates certain problems, such as finding time to manage assets, choosing the right investment strategies, taking care of our belongings, and being very busy working to keep our wealth. Not having money creates a long list of its own problems, such as figuring out how to pay the rent, deciding whether to buy groceries or medicine, worrying about how to save for a child's college education and being very busy working two jobs to keep the family afloat. Whether we have money or not, one thing we all have in common is this: we have problems.

But there's one money-related problem we can all avoid – letting our economic situation influence our family relationships.

Romans 12:16

Live in harmony with one another. Do not be proud, but be willing to associate with people of low position. Do not be conceited.

Avoiding the fight

There's a saying among weightlifters: "No pain, no gain." I'd rather live by this maxim instead: "No pain? Cool! No pain!"

There is one way to avoid having pain in weightlifting. Don't lift weights. But if you don't work out you'll get flabby and weak. Avoiding the pain is not necessarily a good thing. Likewise, it's foolish to stay away from a loved one with whom you've had a disagreement simply because you want to avoid another confrontation.

Few people enjoy fighting. But if you know there is the potential for a fight, the best thing you can do is prepare for it. First, prepare to prevent it from escalating into an argument and have the discussion remain civil and productive. Second, prepare for the possibility that the fight happens anyway. In the case of a broken family relationship in which there is the potential for another fight to erupt when you try to reach out to heal the relationship, planning for the encounter is one way to proactively deal with it. Here's what you do:

1. Pray about the relationship. Ask God to take care of it. Put the problem on His broad shoulders.
2. Think about everything that you want to say and why you want

to say it. Consider the reasons for feeling the way you feel and try to articulate them to yourself.

3. Consider all the reasons that the other person is angry with you. Put yourself in their shoes and try to really understand why they feel the way they do.

4. Pray for understanding. Pray for patience. Pray for guidance. Pray. Ask for help from the greatest healer of all time.

5. Use the 2-1 rule. God gave you two ears and one mouth. You should use your ears twice as much as your mouth. Speak less. Listen more. Hearing someone is the best way to heal the relationship. There'll be plenty of time for you to be heard.

It is easier not to deal with the situation

What can be easier than doing nothing? Nothing! However, doing nothing when something needs attention is irresponsible, foolish, and pointless. You accomplish only one thing when you don't deal with a family separation: you prolong the amount of time that you will suffer the emptiness and sadness that are the inevitable side effects of broken relationships.

If you think that it is easier not to deal with a broken relationship, you are wrong. At best all you do by avoiding the issue is delay the inevitable. At worst you wait too long, and one of you dies. If your loved one dies first, you can be sure that you will feel foolish, heartbroken and helpless as you cry over a corpse or a cold tombstone begging for forgiveness. Don't wait for that to happen. Reach out now!

CHAPTER THREE

Common Themes

If you have experienced or are currently living with a broken relationship, you may be tempted to think that your situation is unique. You may even think that no one could possibly understand your special situation. However, chances are good that no matter what you are going through in a relationship, someone has gone through it before. Moreover, it is likely that someone will go through it after you. There are many common themes among family disputes. Let's look at these one at a time.

Innocent people are trapped in the middle

<u>Genesis 43:29-30</u>

"As he looked about and saw his brother Benjamin, his own mother's son, he asked, "Is this your youngest brother, the one you told me about?" And he said, "God be gracious to you my son." Deeply moved at the site of this brother, Joseph hurried out and looked for a place to weep. He went into his private room and wept there."

In the story of Joseph and his brothers we discover that Benjamin, Joseph's younger brother, becomes a pawn and an unknowing player in the middle of a broken family relationship. Joseph schemed to have his brothers bring Benjamin to him and later planned a way that he could keep Benjamin with him.

<u>*Genesis 44:1-2*</u>:

Now Joseph gave these instructions to the steward of his house: "Fill the men's sacks with as much food as they can carry, and put each man's silver in the mouth of his sack. Then put my cup, the silver one, in the mouth of the youngest one's sack, along with the silver for his grain".

Joseph's intentions may have been good but he used deception to have his brother Benjamin stay with him rather than return to his father, Jacob. Can you imagine the fear that Benjamin might have felt when he was accused of stealing the silver cup that had been purposely placed there on Joseph's order? He knew he was innocent yet he had no way of proving it! And because of Joseph's deception, Benjamin would be made a slave. He must have been frightened; after all, he was only a young boy.

Often times, innocent people – particularly children – are caught in the middle of a family dispute. Torn between the feuding family members, they are forced to choose sides. In family disputes there are always others involved. I have heard of stories of parents even withholding Christmas gifts sent to their children by a family member with whom they are fighting, because they want nothing to do with the person who sent the gift. Praise God that He never holds back His gift of salvation from His children for any reason! Yet the human heart can be so hardened that it wants to spread its anger and hatred to everyone around it. If this is you, pray for forgiveness and pray for the ability to forgive.

If you are involved in a family dispute, look out for the innocent ones. Consider them first. Fix what is broken, if not for yourself then for them. Part of healing the broken relationship includes dealing with those who were affected through no fault of their own. Even if you cannot heal the relationship, you must do everything in your power to minimize the effect on innocent bystanders. God will hold us accountable for the harm we do to the innocent ones around us – especially to children – for Jesus said:

<u>*Luke 18:16-17*</u>

But Jesus called the children to him and said, "Let the little children come to me, and do not hinder them, for the kingdom of God belongs to such as these. I tell you the truth, anyone who will not receive the Kingdom of God like a little child will never enter it."

God help us if we let our family disputes, our pride, our arrogance and our hardened spirit teach our children the virtue of holding a grudge against a loved one rather than exhibiting the spirit of God and learning to forgive and love unconditionally.

We use other people in our disputes

Joseph used his servants to do his dirty work.

<u>Genesis 44:3-5</u>

> *As morning dawned, the men were sent on their way with their donkeys. They had not gone far from the city when Joseph said to the steward, "Go after those men at once, and when you catch up with them, say to them, 'Why have you repaid good with evil? Isn't this the cup my master drinks from and also uses for divination? This is a wicked thing you have done.'"*

Having ordered them to plant the cup in Benjamin's sack, he now sends his men to falsely accuse the youngster of stealing it. The men are ordered to arrest Benjamin and bring him back to the city. Joseph's servants must have wondered what was going on. They must have known that Joseph was setting the boy up, but because they worked for Joseph they had no choice but to be a part of the trap. Similarly, people in family disputes use others to help them deal with those with whom they are fighting. They may send a son or daughter to deliver a message to the family member with whom they don't want to talk. Or they may send a sister or brother to retrieve a family heirloom from the home of another sibling with whom they are fighting. Whatever the case, we have absolutely no right to involve others in our disputes.

Parties involved can be hurt

By definition, a fight includes getting hurt. Bruises and broken bones heal and some blows may not even leave a mark at all. But emotional scars cut deep into the spirit, sometimes leaving gashes that not even time can heal completely. The spiritual hemorrhaging that is caused when family members fight cannot be stopped with conventional medicines or human intervention. Some people try to stop the bleeding with illicit drugs and alcohol, but that only compounds their problems. Or they try to make the pain go away by paying a therapist hundreds of dollars per hour for counseling. Others try to heal their wounds for free by gossiping with friends, their children or other family members. The only real and lasting cure is found with Christ. Asking Him for forgiveness, strength, wisdom, and the willpower to change is the only genuine solution.

Stubborn attitudes seem to prevail

Why is it that people choose to remain angry rather than apologizing and talking about things that must be resolved? When we are angry we always have at least two choices: stop being angry or stay angry. Why do so many people choose the latter? Is it easier to stay angry? Usually, and sadly, the answer is yes. What do we have to do to stay angry? The answer is simple: nothing!

Resolving disputes takes energy. You have to subject yourself to actually listening to the other party and trying to understand their point of view. You have to work hard to articulate your thoughts clearly so that they can be fully understood and well-received. You have to take the time to interact with the people involved, and you have to be willing to change your mind. All in all, most people would rather dig three eight-foot deep graves with a spoon than do any of those things! Digging the graves would be easier for many of us than changing our mind or listening to a differing opinion. But there is only one use for a grave, and that's to bury something. By avoiding the discussion and remaining stubborn and angry, the only grave you are digging is the one you are driving your relationship to.

Ephesians 4:26-27

In your anger do not sin. Do not let the sun go down while you are still angry, and do not give the devil a foothold.

You may not be able to settle a family dispute in a day. Distance or other circumstances may physically separate you and the person you are fighting with; and besides, sometimes a cooling off period is a good thing. However, settling your anger is another matter. In his letter to the Ephesians, Paul is very clear about what we must do with our anger. He warns us not to sin in anger and not to go to bed angry. That means we must pray about why we are angry, and we must pray for the person with whom we are cross. We must ask for forgiveness for our anger and for wisdom on how to deal with it.

When we are no longer irritated, we can begin the process of considering how to best heal the relationship. More than one sunset may pass before we can accomplish that mission, but one thing is certain: *dealing from a position of anger is dealing from a position of weakness.* The other family member may remain angry with you, but to begin the healing process it is imperative that you have already forgiven them in your heart, and that you are willing to work toward healing the relationship. If we are going to be stubborn and wait for someone to apologize to us before we stop being angry we may want to get a bigger spoon because we will be digging that grave!

After a while we forget why we fought

Think back to the last time you were really angry at someone you love. I mean *really* angry. Can you remember exactly why you were angry? What did your loved one do to make you so angry? Can you remember the words that were spoken – who said what to whom, and when? And if your anger has long since past and you still have a wonderful and loving relationship with that person now, what would you say about the reasons for the fight? Would you say they were silly or even funny? Stupid? How about childish? Maybe you would even say that the reasons were not so important after all?

Now consider someone who had a fight with a loved one ten years ago or perhaps even more, and who still remains angry to this day. Perhaps they have neither seen nor spoken to their loved one since their big blowup. How much of what transpired could they really remember? How much of their so called memory has been replaced with their own biased and self-serving view of the fight? Chances are excellent that what they remember is as much fiction as fact. Each time they tell the story – and they always tell the story over and over again – they add something new. They change one word or an inflection in the tone of voice, and each time the story is told it becomes more fantastic and incredible. More often than not each time they tell the story they make themselves look like the victim and the other person the brutal aggressor. Even the witnesses to the fight have different recollections of the events. Who started it? Who used foul language first? Who threw the first punch? Who accused whom? Who wrote the first spiteful letter?

Perhaps a better question is: who cares? Does it really matter who started the fight? What difference does that make now? How will dwelling on these questions move us toward healing? Answering them may help, but dwelling on them will never be beneficial. Can the milk be put back into the glass after it's spilled? Couldn't we just fill the glass with some fresh milk? Think about it. Pray about it. You want to dwell on something? Dwell on the profound stupidity of remaining angry with someone for days, weeks, months, years, or a lifetime. Life is indeed too short!

If you are angry with someone and have been for a long time, it is almost certain that you can't really remember the reasons why. Even if you can remember exactly why you and the other person fought, the reasons are probably not that important any longer. Suppose that you and your brother fought over a girl twenty years ago. And suppose that now each of you has been happily married for the past fifteen years, neither of you having married the girl you fought over. Does the fight over the girl – whose name you may not even be able to remember – still matter? This is an overly simplistic example. But I challenge you to consider the possibility that your reasons for breaking ties with a loved one are simply no longer important. If that's the case, why in the world are you still not talking to them?

Ah, but I know what you're thinking. What if you *do* remember the reasons for fighting with a family member, and those reasons are still important, and you are still angry? What if, even after the passage of time, you still can't help but dwell on the events that led to the fight and all that's happened since. Does this describe you? Then ask yourself these questions: How long will you allow yourself to be unhappy about something? How much of your joyful energy will you allow to be sapped? What do you gain by remaining angry? And now, ask yourself this: Does any of this make sense, or are you just acting foolishly? Before you answer that last question, think! Be honest with yourself; no one else is watching. Well, almost no One!

Finally, if you've come to the conclusion that you can't remember a good reason for the fight or that the reasons just don't matter anymore, there is an outstanding possibility that neither does the person with whom you had the fight. Reach out to them!

Over time, people care less about resolution

Have you heard the old saying that "absence makes the heart grow fonder?" How I wish that was always true! For if it was, it would be impossible for family and friends who once loved one another to remain apart for years. Sadly, absence and the passage of time can also make the heart grow forgetful. We can forget the good times we had with someone. We can forget the times we cried together, laughed together and played together. Not having a relationship with someone becomes normal. It becomes all right. We no longer really miss them. We replace them with other people; neighbors, friends, church family, co-workers and other family members. We fill the time we used to spend with them doing other things, and after a while it seems normal not to have them around. It rarely crosses our mind that we have a sister, a brother, a mother, a father, a daughter, a son, a cousin, an aunt, an uncle, a grandparent or a friend that we have not seen in a very long time. Once in a while we page through an old picture album and someone asks us, "Who is that?" When that happens, we sigh and say, "Someone I knew a long time ago."

Is this you? Call that person! Write to them! Visit them! Hug them! Cry with them again! Rekindle what you once had.

Next generation inherits the problem

What do you think the chances are that the children of feuding family members will have a normal, loving and productive relationship? If you guessed zero percent, you would be right! How could they possibly have a chance at developing such a relationship? The odds are better that they will grow up to be complete strangers who never see or even know of each other. I have a few cousins that I have never met. I have others who I have seen a handful of times in my life. It's tough enough having a reasonable relationship with cousins when there is no family dispute to get in the way, let alone getting to know those with whom I've never had contact.

The last time I saw one of my aunts was at my maternal grandfather's funeral. Then I saw another aunt at my maternal grandmother's funeral. That's it! I have seen my mother's sister five or six times throughout my entire life! Writing this book has convinced me of two things. One, family feuds are part of the family inheritance; and two, only I can change that. If I want to have a relationship with my aunt, I have to make the call. If I want to see and meet my cousins, I have to take the initiative.

Is this the legacy you want to leave for your children and your children's children? Do you want them to think of you as a bitter old person who could not make up with someone in their family? Or do you want them to see the spirit of God working through you and see with their own eyes how it is manifested in forgiveness and love? The choice is yours.

However, what if your children don't know their family members not because of your unwillingness to get back together, but because of the other person's desire to have no contact with you? What then? Do you simply say, "Oh well, I tried," and let it go at that? Not at all. In this case you must talk with your children about the situation and encourage them to seek their own relationships with the family member. You may even facilitate interaction by driving the children to a place where they can meet their relative. Encourage them to write letters and e-mails and to make phone calls. Urge them to pray for their family member. Do everything in your power to prevent your broken relationship from interfering with their ability to build productive relationships of their own. Who knows – these interactions may be the spring thaw that melts the ice around the family member with whom you are feuding. It may be that healing begins through those innocent relationships initiated by your children. Or it may be the relationship that you continue to have with the other person's spouse that eventually reopens the channels of communication.

Do you want to leave your family members something upon your passing? Leave them money. Leave them the house. Leave behind some jewelry. And by all means, leave behind that classic Harley Davidson. Most of all, leave them a legacy that causes them to remember you with pride.. Let them remember you as someone who lived a good Christian life, who did his best to further the kingdom of God and who loved his neighbor – including, and especially, his family members!

<u>*Matthew 25:21*</u>

His Master replied, "Well done, good and faithful servant! You have been faithful with a few things; I will put you in charge of many things. Come and share your master's happiness!"

Let these be the words that God speaks when we stand before him in judgment – not, *"Now explain to me again why you refused to get back together with your Dad?"*

CHAPTER FOUR

What Keeps Us Apart?

I struggled for a long time to come up with the words to open this chapter. There is no easy way to tell someone that they are being stupid or that foolish pride is preventing them from seeing the issues clearly. It's hard to tell a person that they are behaving arrogantly or in a self-centered way. It's never easy to confront someone with the truth about his or her hardened spirit, unforgiving attitude or disregard for all the innocent people affected by their ridiculous behavior. These are tough things to acknowledge and come to terms with. Yet, what else could explain why some people don't even try to get back together with their family members? No doubt we can come up with an exhaustive list of reasons – or should we call them *excuses*? While a good reason may pop up now and then, it's difficult to imagine one that could not be overcome.

In this chapter we will explore some of the reasons why family members stay apart after there has been a fight. The Bible provides clear guidance for what we should do about them. I'll warn you up front: the truth hurts. If you are involved in a family dispute and you are not trying to fix it – whether you feel you started it or not – you will be convicted by what the Bible has to say. Brave souls who want to heal relationships, read on.

Stupidity

Webster's Dictionary defines stupid this way:

stu-pid: 1a: slow of mind, obtuse. b: given to unintelligent decisions or acts: acting in an unintelligent or careless manner. c: lacking intelligence or reason. 2: dulled in feeling or sensation. 3: marked by or resulting from unreasoned thinking or acting.

Is there anyone who understands the meaning of the word and who likes being called stupid? Nevertheless, think back to some of the arguments that you've had in the past. Given the benefit of hindsight, how many of them would you say fit the definition of "stupid?" I know from personal experience that many of the arguments I have been involved in have been dumb ones. We often fight over things that in reality are quite silly. Imagine a fight erupting between the fathers of two young boys playing an ice hockey game – a fight that leads to one man literally punching the other to death in front of all the children? Unfortunately that is exactly what happened at an ice rink in Massachusetts. Now, two young boys are without their fathers, one because his dad is dead and the other because his dad is in jail for manslaughter! Who would argue the supreme stupidity of that fight? Who would defend the behavior of either person, especially given the horrific result?

Why is it that this type of thing happens so often? It happens in white families and black families, in Christian homes and Jewish homes, in rich families and poor families. It happens between family members who are well educated and between those who never finished school. No one is immune. We all seem to have an extraordinary and innate ability to act stupid from time to time.

The more I think about this, the more convinced I am that occasional fighting among family members is unavoidable. It's going to happen now and then no matter how hard we try to keep ours emotions and temper in check. Being able to forgive and make up however, is completely within our control.

We must ensure that we are not acting stupidly and preventing our relationships from being healed. We must accept correction from those who advise us, and we must be convicted by our own actions. Here's what the Bible has to say about it:

Proverbs 12:1:

Whoever loves discipline loves knowledge, but he who hates correction is stupid.

<u>2 Timothy 2:23</u>:

Don't have anything to do with foolish and stupid arguments,
because you know they produce quarrels.

Pray that we are not acting stupidly in dealing with broken relationships. Pray that you will accept correction and make wise decisions based on logical, sound thinking.

Pride

According to *Webster*:

<u>pride</u>: 1: the quality or state of being proud: a: inordinate self-esteem: CONCEIT: b: a reasonable or justifiable self-respect c: delight or elation arising from some act, possession or relationship. 2: proud or disdainful behavior or treatment: DISDAIN: 3: a: ostentatious display.

How's that for a word with many different meanings? Pride is one of those words that can have a good or a bad connotation. Depending on the context of its use, the word pride can be a compliment or an insult. It can refer to a person's greatest quality or one of their greatest character flaws.

"I'm so proud of you," a father says to his daughter. That's good pride. "I'm proud to be an American." That too is good pride.

"I'm proud to be a part of this team." "I wear my Air Force uniform proudly." "He stands tall and proud because of his accomplishments." These are all examples of healthy pride.

"He is so proud that he can't bring himself to apologize." "Her pride was hurt and now she does not want to speak to me." "He's acting conceited because of his pride." These are examples of bad pride.

Here's the tough part: there is a fine line between good and bad pride. To be sure that you are not allowing foolish pride to get in the way of rebuilding relationships, give your behavior the Humble Test, otherwise known as the WWJD Test. You've seen kids wearing bracelets printed with the acronym *WWJD*, haven't you? Those initials stand for

What Would Jesus Do? and they remind us to ask ourselves that question whenever a sticky situation arises and we don't know what to do. Apply the test to your behavior within your family's dispute, and ask yourself, "Would Jesus act as I am acting? Would I act this way if Jesus was standing next to me right now?"

Guess what? He is!

<u>Proverbs 16:5</u>

The Lord detests all the proud of heart. Be sure of this: They will not go unpunished.

I realize that I will have much explaining to do once I stand before God in judgment, but I pray that I won't have to spend any time trying to justify my "bad" pride. The above passage from Proverbs makes it crystal clear that God has a special disdain for the proud of heart, and for good reason. Pride often separates us from our loved ones – the same loved ones that God gave to us to cherish and share our lives with. Don't let pride get in your way of healing a relationship with someone you love!

Arrogance

<u>1 Samuel 2:3</u>

Do not keep talking so proudly or let your mouth speak such arrogance, for the Lord is a God who knows, and by him deeds are weighed.

<u>Proverbs 21:24</u>

The proud and arrogant man – 'Mocker' is his name; he behaves with overweening pride.

Look up the word arrogance in a thesaurus and you will find words such as overbearing pride, haughtiness, presumption, loftiness, imperviousness, vanity, conceit, self-importance, contempt, and scorn.

Arrogance can be displayed in many ways, including:

+ Not listening to others
+ Interrupting others while they are speaking
+ Dismissing ideas because of the source rather than considering the idea's merit
+ Being impolite or rude
+ Being insensitive to people's feelings
+ Expecting special treatment

The list can go on and on. What do all of these misdeeds have in common? They are overt behaviors – behaviors that people can see, feel and hear. The actual words used are not necessarily the issue; it can be how they are said that counts. Body language or the way a person walks can express arrogance to others. True arrogance is founded on the person's profound (and mistaken) belief that they are better than other people. It may be by virtue of their education, the school they attended, their socio-economic status, their job title or some expertise that causes the arrogant person to consider themselves superior to others. That belief, manifested in actual behaviors, is the embodiment of arrogance.

Sometimes our own arrogance can blind us. Arrogance can make a person feel invincible and incapable of being wrong. Here's a news flash – everyone is vulnerable, and everyone can be wrong. Just ask my wife!

Not surprisingly, arrogance and pride are often intertwined. Frank Koch of the Naval Institute wrote the following short story of a ship's captain and how his arrogance blinded him, nearly costing him his ship:

> Two battleships assigned to the training squadron had been at sea on maneuvers in heavy weather for several days. I was serving, on the lead battleship and was on watch on the bridge as night fell. The visibility was poor with patchy fog, so the captain remained on the bridge keeping an eye on all activities. Shortly after dark, the lookout on the wing of the bridge reported, "Light, bearing on the starboard bow."

> "Is it steady or moving astern?" the captain called out.

> Lookout replied, "Steady captain," which meant we were on a dangerous collision course with that ship.

The captain then called to the signalman, "Signal that ship: We are on a collision course, advise you change your course 20 degrees."

Back came a signal, "Advisable for you to change course 20 degrees."

The captain said, "Send, I'm a captain, change course 20 degrees."

"I'm a seaman second class," came the reply. "You had better change course 20 degrees."

By that time, the captain was furious. He spat out, "Send, I'm a battleship. Change course 20 degrees."

Back came the flashing light, "I'm a lighthouse."

We changed our course.

If we are not careful, we can allow our arrogance and pride to steer our relationship directly into the path of an iceberg the same way this captain almost blindly wrecked his ship into a lighthouse. We will not realize the iceberg's size since most of it is hidden below the surface – just like many of our family issues. There they sit, waiting to tear through the hull of our relationship and sink our family into a murky and churning sea. There is no room in our lives and our family relationships for unhealthy pride or arrogance. Pray for a humble spirit. Pray that arrogance and pride will not get in the way of having productive, strong and happy relationships with those we love.

Self-Centeredness

In my book *The Legacy Leader*, I addressed the character flaws that leaders must work to eliminate. As it relates to self-centeredness, I wrote:

For a leader, adjectives starting with "self" can signify positive or negative traits for him or her to possess. Self-control, self-confidence, and self-assurance are excellent traits for a leader. Selfish, self-reliant, and self-satisfied, on the other hand, are among the negative ones. Probably the worst trait in the "self" category is self-centeredness. A self-centered leader is one who is swellheaded, vain and immodest; someone who practices self-love – not the healthy sense of worth that we should all have for ourselves – but rather a preoccupation with our own self-interest that negatively impacts others. This negative form of self-love goes to the core of arrogance, which we already stated was the first of the cardinal character sins for a leader... The Legacy Leader must strive to replace self-centeredness with self-esteem, self-respect, independence, self-regard, confidence, and pardonable pride. The fine line between pardonable pride and arrogant pride is humility. Being proud, confident, self-assured and in control while maintaining a humble spirit does not mean that the leader is meek, weak or quirky. It simply means that they don't need to boast, strut, and pound on their chest like King Kong in order to get everybody's attention.

All of us – not only leaders – have to ensure that our behaviors are not self-centered and self-serving, especially as it relates to our family relationships. When it comes to family we must have a servant heart and spirit. We must want *to please* more than *to be pleased*. We must want what's best for them rather than what's best for ourselves. This is difficult to do! Often there is no progress made in healing broken relationships because no one is willing to budge from their own self-serving point of view. So they stand at one end of the battle field with arms folded and refuse to take a step forward, while we stand at the other end doing the same, both insisting that the other party make the first move.

See you at the wake!

Here's what the Bible has to say about being self-centered:

Romans 2:7-8

To those who by persistence in doing good seek glory, honor, and immortality, he will give eternal life. But to those who

> *are self-seeking and who reject the truth and follow evil, there will be wrath and anger.*

Any questions? Pray that you will not be self-centered in your family relationships.

A Hardened Spirit

Proverbs 28:14

> *Blessed is the man who always fears the Lord, but he who hardens his heart falls into trouble.*

There are five characteristics of people with hardened hearts: they don't listen, they are stubborn, they can be easily fooled, it takes a major event to finally break them down, and sometimes, even after they have dealt with their hardened attitude, they can become hardened again very quickly.

One of the best examples of how a person with a hardened spirit can act – even in the face of painful and negative outcomes – is depicted in the Book of Exodus.

Exodus 7:13

> *Yet Pharaoh's heart became hard and he would not listen to them, just as the Lord had said.*

In the Book of Exodus we learn how Moses, following God's orders, goes before the Pharaoh to demand the Hebrews' release from slavery. But Pharaoh's heart was hardened, and he would not listen to Moses. Thus, the first thing we learn about someone with a hardened heart is that they can't listen! There are many things that can get in a way of having a conversation with someone, but the most significant roadblock to meaningful discussions is someone's inability to listen. You can forget about healing a relationship if you cannot communicate. Since listening is a key element in communication, if you can't listen, you can't heal. So the first step is to deal with your hardened heart if you want to have a chance at fixing a broken relationship with your loved one.

<u>*Exodus 7:14-16*</u>

Then the Lord said to Moses, "Pharaoh's heart is unyielding;
he refuses to let the people go. Go to Pharaoh in the morning
as he goes out to the water. Wait on the bank of the Nile to
meet him, and take in your hand the staff that was changed
into a snake. Then say to him, 'The Lord, the God of the
Hebrews, has sent me to say to you: Let my people go, so
that they may worship me in the desert. But until now you
have not listened.'"

The second thing we learn about a hardened heart is that it is a
stubborn heart! Pharaoh is about to learn the hard way what the result
of a hardened heart can be.

<u>*Exodus 7:20-21*</u>

Moses and Aaron did just as the Lord had commanded. He
raised his staff in the presence of the Pharaoh and his officials
and struck the water of the Nile and all the water changed
into blood. The fish of the Nile died, and the river smelled so
bad that the Egyptians could not drink its water. Blood was
everywhere in Egypt.

I don't know about you, but if I saw a river turn into blood before
my eyes I would definitely be frightened into submission. But that's not
necessarily the nature of a hardened heart. In fact, the opposite often
occurs. When people with hardened hearts are faced with the truth and
are challenged to deal with it, they can become increasingly calloused and
resistant. That is precisely what happened with Pharaoh. It would take
several plagues and even fire from heaven to get him to listen. There was
the plague of frogs, followed by the plague of gnats, then flies, livestock,
boils, hail, locusts, and the plague of darkness. Each time, Pharaoh had
a chance to change his mind and let the Hebrews go. Each time, he
promised that he would comply, but only long enough to make the plague
stop. As soon as the plague ceased, however, he hardened his heart again
and changed his mind about freeing the Hebrews.

Perhaps the reason he changed his mind was that his court magicians

– through trickery, no doubt – could duplicate what Moses had done with his staff.

But the Egyptian magicians did the same things by their secret arts, and Pharaoh's heart became hardened; he would not listen to Moses and Aaron, just as the LORD had said..

These charlatans lulled Pharaoh into a false sense of security. They figured out a way to show him what he wanted to see. These days we would refer to them as "yes men." These are folks who will tell their friends, leaders, bosses, or others only what they think these people want to hear. They want to remain in good standing with the person, so rather than telling them the truth they lie and say all the right things, every time.

We're all surrounded by people like this, people who would prefer to pacify us with the easy things rather than tell us the hard truth. Some people would happily feed our hardened spirit and tell us that we are right to be angry with our family member for having wronged us. They not only feed our anger but they also help us feel righteous in our position as the victim in a broken relationship. Few people are willing to do the right thing and challenge us to face what the Bible has to say about anger and love, or about dealing with our brothers and sisters. Few people will do for us what Nathan did for David. Nathan rebuked David for having stolen Bathsheba from Uriah.

Nathan went to David and told him a story about a rich man who had stolen from a poor man. Having heard the story, David was angry and told Nathan that this rich man should be severely punished. Imagine David's surprise when Nathan said to him:

2 Samuel 12:7-10

"Then Nathan said to David, you are the man! This is what the Lord, the God of Israel, says: 'I anointed you king over Israel, and I delivered you from the hand of Saul. ⁸I gave your master's house to you, and your master's wife into your

arms. I gave you the house of Israel and Judah. And if all of
this had been too little, I would have given you even more.
⁹Why did you despise the word of the Lord by doing what is
evil in His eyes? You struck down Uriah the Hittite with the
sword and took his wife to be your own. You killed him with
the sword of the Ammonites. ¹⁰ Now, therefore, the sword
will never depart from your house, because you despised me
and took the wife of Uriah the Hittite to be your own."

Like Pharaoh, we too can be deceived and misled by people who
would offer advice on how not to deal with our broken relationships but
rather how to remain angry and distant from our family members. Pray
for a Nathan in your life, someone who will help you soften your heart
so you can deal with your broken relationship. And pray for a Nathan in
your family member's life as well, so that they can also be softened. Only
then can the healing begin.

Sadly it often takes something rather significant to humble and
break us before we come to our senses and soften our spirit.

Exodus 11:4-6

So Moses said, "This is what the Lord says: 'About midnight,
I will go throughout Egypt. Every firstborn son in Egypt will
die, from the firstborn of Pharaoh, who sits on the throne,
to the firstborn son of the slave girl, who is at her hand mill,
and all the firstborn of the cattle as well. There will be loud
wailing throughout Egypt – worse than there has ever been
or ever will be again.'"

Pharaoh was about to lose his son because of his arrogant and
hardened spirit! Why does it take something this serious to get our
attention? Why should it take the death of a family member, a serious
illness or some other catastrophic event before we soften our hearts? Can
we afford to be that stubborn? Pray now that God will soften your heart
and that it will not take a major event like Pharaoh's before you see the
light and do something to restore your family relationships.

After the Passover when Pharaoh finally broke down and let the
Hebrews go, it wasn't long before he changed his mind again.

<u>*Exodus 14:8*</u>

The Lord hardened the heart of the Pharaoh King of Egypt, so that he pursued the Israelites, who were marching out boldly.

It is sad that people – all of us in fact – tend to sink back into sin! Wouldn't it be nice if, after asking God for forgiveness for our sins, He would forgive us and we would never do it again? That is simply not our nature. We are sinful people. And for those who have a tendency to have a hardened spirit, it takes special work and prayer to remain humbled and soft-spirited.

Unforgiving attitude

Take a quick glance at the words *forgiveness, forgive, forgiving, forget,* and *forgot* in the subject index of any Bible and you will find more than one hundred scripture verses that refer directly to these terms. We have all needed to be forgiven for something that we've done, and we have all forgiven someone else for something they did to us. Yet most of us have limits to our forgiveness. There are some things that fall into our "unforgivable" category.

Have you ever heard someone say, "I could never forgive them for that." Perhaps you've even said it yourself. This is one of the common themes in broken relationships. Yet in the Bible, God gives no clearer direction on any other subject than He does on forgiveness – on seeking it and granting it.

Perhaps the best way to understand what it means to have a forgiving attitude is to examine how we are forgiven by God. God's grace is unbounded and He can forgive us any sin! There is no one that has as great a forgiving attitude as He. Forgiveness is easy to get but it is not automatic. Through Christ Jesus every person has the opportunity to receive forgiveness, but it does not happen without us asking for it. There are several Bible verses that help us understand the process of forgiveness:

<u>*1 John 1:9*</u>

If we confess our sins, He is faithful and just to forgive us our sins, and to cleanse us from all unrighteousness.

Thus the first thing we must do is confess our sins. The next step is to turn away from what caused us to sin and need forgiveness in the first place.

Ezekiel 18:21

But if a wicked man turns away from all the sins he has committed and keeps all my decrees and does what is just and right, he will surely live; he will not die.

If we are sincere in our repentant heart and ask God for forgiveness, it follows that we should seek forgiveness from those we have wronged. Finally, the last step in seeking forgiveness from God is to "fix" situations where we failed in our responsibilities to others.

Romans 13:7

Give everyone what you owe him: If you owe taxes, pay taxes; if revenue, then revenue; if respect, then respect; if honor, then honor.

Sincere repentance is accompanied by action. This action means that we pay back what we've done wrong; whether it's paying back with money, material things, or words. If you have wronged someone it is up to you to apologize and then work to make it right. No one can do this for you.

The reward for seeking forgiveness is freedom from the bondage of guilt. However just as God forgives us, He expects us to forgive our brothers and sisters. When Peter asked Jesus how many times he was to forgive his brothers, Jesus answered:

Matthew 18:22

… I tell you, not seven times, but seventy-seven times.

We are also promised this:

Matthew 6:14-15

¹⁴For if you forgive men when they sin against you, your

> *heavenly Father will also forgive you.* [15]*But if you do not forgive men their sins, your Father will not forgive your sins.*

Not only are we instructed to forgive over and over again, but we are warned that we should not expect forgiveness if we are unwilling to give it. If we receive God's forgiveness, we are bound to forgive others. Forgiveness is something to be practiced daily. There is nothing that we ought not to be able to forgive. As difficult as this sounds and as completely unpractical as it may appear, this is what we are instructed to strive for.

As the father of two beautiful girls and the husband of a beautiful and terrific wife, I am always very disturbed when I see a news report about a little child victimized or killed by some idiot. It's sad enough when a child dies as a result of an accident or a terrible disease, but there is a special sting to the death when it's at the hand of someone with an evil and senseless purpose. I am just as disturbed when I hear a report of a wife beaten by her husband or raped by some animal on the street. In my heart I've always wondered if I could ever forgive someone who did that to my children or my wife. I don't know if I would have the strength to love them the way God does. Yet that is what He commands. He commands us to have a forgiving attitude. As bad as things may seem between you and your feuding family member, God has made it clear that you are to seek forgiveness and grant forgiveness to them.

We can come up with dozens of excuses for not forgiving someone. We can rationalize that they will never change, or that they'll just cross us again in the future. We may believe that they are not really sorry for what they did to us. Unfortunately, that may all be true. However, your responsibility is to forgive them anyway. God will deal with the rest.

Disregard for other innocent people affected

If there's a "worst case scenario" among the categories of broken family relationships, I suppose the breakdown of a marriage would be at the top of the list. In today's society, divorce is a fast way out of a difficult, unpleasant and inconvenient situation. Sadly, more than half of all marriages in the United States end in divorce. And even more sadly, it is often the children of the marriage that are most adversely affected by the breakdown. The scars that can be left on the children of divorced parents can affect the rest of their lives. Without doubt, one of the primary lessons that children of divorced parents learn is that when a relationship isn't working, you can simply break it off and go your separate ways. After all, if Mom and Dad did it, why can't I?

Other types of family breakdowns affect innocent bystanders as well. When grown sisters with children of their own fight and don't see each other, it means that the cousins don't see each other either – ever again! When grown brothers with sons of their own shut each other out, it means that their boys get the message that it's just fine not to talk to loved ones anymore after a fight. When a daughter decides that she no longer wants to see her father, she denies her children the right to know their grandfather. When a son decides that he will no longer speak to his mother, he teaches his kids that one day it will be okay if they don't let him see *his* grandchildren anymore.

Children learn their behaviors from us. If they see us drink, then it will be okay for them to drink. If they hear us curse, then that will be fine for them, too. If we smoke, we might as well buy the baby an ashtray because she will probably need one eventually. If we read the Bible, our kids will want to follow our example and read it for themselves. If we go to church, they will take their kids to church. If we tell them we love them, they will tell their kids that they love them, too. If we fight with our sister and say that we never want to see her again, we've opened the door for our kids to do exactly the same thing.

You can rest assured that if you are fighting with a family member, you are impacting the innocent people around you. You are sending lifelong messages. You are creating a legacy that will live on long after you are dead. You are ensuring that the dysfunction you are suffering in your own relationships will be passed on to your kids, nephews, nieces, sisters, brothers and friends. Quite a lousy bequest, wouldn't you say?

A few more excuses

There are at least three more reasons why family members stop seeing each other. Actually, they are better referred to as *excuses* rather than *reasons*. They are time, not wanting to deal with difficult issues, and distance.

There is never enough time for us to do everything we want to do.

Schedules are busy enough as it is. And since we know that a reunion with our feuding loved one will force us to deal with a difficult situation, it is easy to convince ourselves that we just don't have the time. It's especially easy to convince ourselves of this when there is physical distance between us and the family member with whom we are estranged. But our God is not a God of excuses; He is a God of action! He is not interested in why we won't make time to fix the problem. He is not interested in hearing about how we are afraid to deal with our brother or sister. He does not care that there are a few miles separating us. He only cares that we did nothing about it.

Make the time! Deal with the tough issue. Take the trip. If not for yourself, do it for the others who are affected by your estranged relationship. Set aside your anger. Stop being so stubborn! Time is ticking away and each second you wait is a second wasted. This is not a dress rehearsal. This is your life, and you only get one shot at it. Let's work to get it right!

What brings family members back together?

Now that we understand the things that keep family members from fixing their broken relationships, let's look at what helps to bring them back together. Regrettably, it often starts with the death of a loved one.

The death of another close relative

Nothing seems to bring people back together quicker than the death of someone in the family. I've met many cousins that I never knew I had at the funerals for my grandmother and grandfather on my mother's side. The relationships between my mom and her sisters, uncles, and even her father were always strained at best. Sadly, the family was quite dysfunctional and distant. It was during the funerals of my grandfather in 1989 and my grandmother in 1995 that my mother last saw her sisters. They talked. They cried. They even hugged. No doubt this scene repeats itself many times each day in many families around the world. These difficult times bring people together, albeit for a brief period of truce. But unless they come together with forgiving attitudes and a prayerful desire to have true healing, the effects of the truce will be short lived. After the grieving for the deceased family member is done, the feud will resume and continue to devastate the lives of all those affected by it.

Serious illness of one of the "combatants"

Sometimes people who have been feuding have a chance to come together before it's too late. It happens when one of the people involved in the fight becomes gravely ill and is hospitalized. Hospital rooms have been the setting for much impromptu family reconciliation. There can be no sadder moment in a person's life than when they are lying in a hospital bed, not only coming to terms with their own mortality but also realizing that they have wasted precious time feeling anger and bitterness toward someone who hurt them – someone they have loved all along. Or perhaps they finally realize that they have been too stubborn to ask for forgiveness from someone they hurt.

Suddenly, now that they find themselves in a hospital bed with tubes and wires coming out of their body, they can't think of one good reason why they waited so long to extend the olive branch! So they beg God for a second chance. They pray like they have never prayed before, asking to be granted enough time to make up with their brother or their sister. They cry out for God to heal them so they can repair the broken relationship with their son or daughter. They beg for the chance to hold their mother or father one last time and tell them they are sorry, before it's too late.

You can't see that happening to you? You can't picture a time when you will feel this way about the broken relationships in your life? Look again. Look harder!

Illness of someone close to the "warriors"

As in the case when one of the feuding family members becomes gravely ill, the illness of someone they are both close to – such as a parent or a sibling – can also bring them back together. Once again the hospital room becomes the setting for a dramatic and tear-jerking scene in which brothers make up after years of fighting. It becomes the setting for sisters to agree that their fight was stupid, and to pledge to do what it takes to restore their relationship.

Unfortunately, it can also be the place where the fighting becomes even more pronounced and profound.

A good friend of mine once told me the story of two brothers who had been fighting for years. When their father was near death in the hospital, he called for his two sons to come visit with him in his room. They stood one on each side of the bed and listened to their father as he made his dying request. He wanted his sons to make up and to "be brothers" again. Amazingly, they denied him that request. He died shortly thereafter, no doubt brokenhearted. Incredible!

Are you as shocked as I that these two brothers could deny their dying father his last request? That they could be so angry, stubborn, hard-hearted, arrogant, and stupid? My goodness – you would think they could have at least faked it for a while, even if only for the benefit of their dying father. Couldn't they put their anger aside until after the funeral? But that is the nature of an unyielding, hardened, stubborn spirit. Only someone with a heart of stone could deny their dying father his final request – and here we meet two of them. Wow!

Will it take the dying request of someone you love to compel you to make up with your sister or brother? God forbid!

One of the people in the feud says "enough"

Sometimes, one party to a feud has an experience that causes them to finally say *enough is enough*. Perhaps they were convicted by their priest's rousing sermon one Sunday morning, or they were deeply touched by a movie that reminded them of their own broken relationship. Maybe they read something that made them finally realize that it's time to get serious about healing the wounds. Or maybe they saw a friend lose her sister to cancer and heard her say how sorry she was that she did not try to fix their relationship sooner. Whatever the reasons, the sooner you decide to wave the white flag, the better!

CHAPTER FIVE

Creating Reconciliation

What is reconciliation? It comes from the word reconcile, which *Webster* defines like this:

> *rec-on-cile*: 1 a: to restore to friendship or harmony. b: settle, resolve (differences) 2 : to make consistent or congruous. 3: to cause to submit to or accept something unpleasant 4: a: to check (a financial account) against another for accuracy b: to account for.

The end goal for reconciliation is harmony. It is the resolution of differences. But note the part of the definition that refers to "submitting to or accepting something unpleasant." To be reconciled with someone does not mean that we will be completely satisfied with them. It does not mean that all of their behaviors, traits, and idiosyncrasies will no longer be an issue for us. It certainly does not mean that we will suddenly have a relationship that is perfect and that we will not have any future disagreements with them. What it does mean is that we will settle our differences to reestablish harmony.

Settling our differences may mean that we accept certain personality traits, points of view and behaviors that we don't necessarily appreciate. While we aren't called upon to compromise on points that violate our most profound beliefs, personal values and integrity, we must be open to accepting the beliefs and values of others.

Before feuding family members can experience true reconciliation, there are some important steps that must be taken to pave the road for this to occur. Let's look at them one at a time.

Seek forgiveness from each other. Not one or the other – but both. But one must go first!

"She started it!"
"I didn't do anything!"
"I'm going to tell mom what you did."
"It's not my fault!"
"Say you're sorry!"
"I'll say I'm sorry if you say it first."

Sound familiar? If you are a parent, I'm certain you've heard all that before. Kids learn to say these things shortly after they learn to say "mommy" and "daddy." They seem cute when you stop to think about it. Childish things can be cute sometimes – when they are done by children. However, childish behaviors are never cute when it's grown people acting that way.

What do we do with kids when they get into these silly arguments? We force them both to apologize to each other. We make sure they each say they are sorry, and we tell them to play nice with one another. That usually works. Ten minutes after what the children thought was the end of the world, they are back at play as if nothing ever happened. Not so with adults. When adults start a silly and sometimes childish argument, there is no one around to pull them both by an ear and order them to play nice together. Why is it that one of these grown people can't realize what's happening and simply be the first to extend the olive branch and apologize?

What do we expect when we extend an apology? Have you ever had an apology not accepted? That rarely happens. Almost every time a sincere apology is extended, it's accepted; and when appropriate it is reciprocated. The result is that both people end up apologizing, but one had to have the courage to take the first step!

I am reminded of a joke:

It seemed that Berny wanted to win the lottery. Each night he prayed to God and he said:

"God, this is one of your favorite sons, Berny. Please let me win the lottery. If you let me win the lottery I will give 25% of the winnings to the church."

Each day, week after week, month after month and year after year, Berny would faithfully pray this prayer to God. One day, Berny changed his prayer. He prayed:

"God, this is one of your favorite sons, Berny. Please let me win the lottery. If you let me win the lottery I will give 50% of the winnings to the church!"

Suddenly a thundering voice came from heaven and exclaimed: "Berny, give me a break and help me out here! Buy a ticket!"

God wants to help us. God *will* help us. But we also need to help ourselves. If there's an apology that needs to happen, don't wait for the other person to step up to the plate. Take the initiative and do it yourself. Chances are good that they feel the same way you do, and like you they let fear, pride, arrogance and their stubborn attitudes get in the way of making the first move.

In most cases, when one member of the family starts by making an apology, it has a tenderizing effect on the others' hearts and opens the way for them to also say they are sorry. Then the healing can begin.

What if the other person remains unmoved and decides not to apologize, or worse yet, they do not respond at all when you hold out an olive branch? Then you simply make it clear to them that you are open to talking with them whenever they are ready. Don't apologize expecting that the other person will reciprocate. That's not the reason to do it. The right reasons for apologizing are:

1. God expects us to
2. It will liberate us from the bondage of guilt
3. It will clear the way for the healing to begin
4. We can then spend time focusing on the next steps rather than worrying about the apology

Words spoken in anger must be forgotten

Think for a moment of words that you have spoken in anger to someone you love. Were some of them hurtful? Did you regret saying them? Did you want to just kick yourself for letting them leave your mouth? Did you really mean them?

153

It is never a good idea to speak words in anger. Yet it seems that part of the human condition includes the uncanny ability to say exactly the wrong thing at precisely the wrong moment. Many of us are masters of this skill. We've also mastered the art of the snappy comeback. That's the finely honed skill of being able to immediately fire an angry comment back in the general direction of the person who just launched one at us. Sometimes we hit our target with pinpoint accuracy. Other times our remarks have a shotgun effect and we fling our bitter words over anything and anyone in the vicinity, including innocent children, other family members and even pets.

Wouldn't it be great if we could control our every emotion and our every word? Wouldn't it be wonderful if you never spoke another word that you needed to apologize for? Sadly, the chances of this happening are slim to none. So we have to settle for the next best thing. We must learn to say we are sorry for words spoken in anger, and we must learn to forgive those who spoke angry words to us.

Try saying these words: *"I'm sorry for what I said. It was dumb and inconsiderate of me. I was angry with you and I couldn't think of anything smart to say. So rather than trying to deal with what I was angry about, I said things that I did not really mean. It must have made you feel terrible to hear me say all that. I love you and I'm sorry for what I said. Please forgive me."*

Only after both sides have issued similar apologies can the communication start to uncover and deal with the real underlying issues. We must learn to forget words spoken toward us by an angry person. That does not mean that we should forget to deal with what caused the anger however, because *that's* what really needs fixing!

Rehashing the past does no good

It's water under the bridge.
No sense in crying over spilled milk.
We have all heard those expressions before. There are probably dozens of sayings that people from all around the world use to mean precisely the same thing: what's done is done. The milk is now just a messy puddle on the floor, and the water that has passed under the bridge cannot come back upstream. It's gone and it does not matter anymore. We use these sayings when we want to express our desire to move on. We don't need to worry about what happened in the past.

Rehashing, reliving, and perpetuating the negative things that happened to us in the past can only accomplish one thing – it allows us to stay angry over something that we should have gotten over a long time ago. How silly is that? How foolish to allow our anger to consume us this way! Anger is debilitating. The more we feed it, the more it demands. The more we harbor it, the more it takes over our every waking moment. If you are angry with someone, ask yourself these questions: How often do you think about it each day? How often do you discuss it with someone else, someone who perhaps shares your anger? How much of your day do you waste by thinking about and fretting over this anger? If you add up all the time you've wasted being angry, and added all the minutes, hours and days that you have spent on the phone talking with someone about how angry you were, you'd probably be amazed. For people who have been angry with someone for years, the wasted energy and time are staggering.

Resolve today that you will not worry about the water under the bridge anymore. Make a commitment to yourself that you are not going to let your anger consume you. Make a courageous decision that enough is enough, and regain control over your life. If the family member you fought with wants to stay angry, pray for them. Pray that God will take their anger away as He has done with yours. Let them know you are no longer angry, and that you are ready to move on with the relationship. Wipe up that sour spilled milk, and pour yourself a tall, fresh glass!

Focus on the present and the future

Although there is clearly nothing we can do to change the past, we can influence our present and, albeit to a lesser degree, our future. I have always been impressed with people who have the ability to live for the moment. They seem carefree and less stressed by the daily routines than the rest of us. They enjoy the moment in which they are living. That does not mean that they don't care about their future, but they don't worry incessantly about it. And if they don't fret over their future too much, they certainly do not worry about the past in the least.

When it comes to personal and family relationships, there can be no better rule than to focus on the present and plan for the future. If you focus on the present, you'll enjoy it more. When you focus on the present even trivial things can take on a new meaning. Walking down to the corner store for a gallon of milk can have meaning if you walk side by side with someone you love and spend the time speaking with them.

I recall a cold autumn day many years ago when my dad and I were outside raking up what seemed like millions of leaves. We talked and raked for a couple of hours. I realized, as I am sure he did, that the time we spent together was quality time. Since then I have come to really appreciate the time with my dad. We install ceiling fans and work on mowers together. We hang sheetrock and paint walls together. But the work is not the fun part. Doing it together is! Those moments can never be taken away from us. The memories we create are everlasting. Focusing on the present is the best way to ensure a past that you can remember fondly. After all, that is what the past is for – to be remembered, not to be lived in.

Focusing on the present also helps create a more hopeful and wonderful future. While we can't be assured of the future, we can do our best to prepare for it. That's what retirement plans are all about. The only thing we know for sure about our future is that we will die someday, and death may come suddenly and unrepentantly. What a shame to waste a single moment of our short lives on this earth worrying about the past, fighting with someone we love, or obsessing about a future that may never come. Instead we should work to strengthen our family bonds today and prepare to enjoy healthy and happy relationships for as long as we live. Now that's a great retirement plan!

Deal with the rift's underlying causes

Thus far in this chapter we've outlined needs to be in place for true reconciliation to happen. We've discussed the importance of forgiveness and dealing with anger. We concluded that rehashing the past is futile. We decided that focusing on the present is the best way to enjoy healthy relationships today. While all of these are essential, dealing with the underlying issues that caused the rift and separation in the first place are of paramount importance. This is where it gets dicey. By comparison, forgiving is easy. Deciding not to worry about the past is totally within your control too, as is consciously choosing to focus on the present. However, acknowledging, understanding and resolving each of the issues that caused a family meltdown is hard work.

Psychiatrists and psychologists have made fortunes charging hourly rates from people who seek their help in dealing with their emotional baggage and broken relationships. I believe doctors can and do help. I believe people should not hesitate to seek professional help when necessary. However, I also believe that the supreme psychiatrist, psychologist, physician, heart and soul surgeon, and ultimate healer is God. The best news is that His services are one hundred percent guaranteed and they are completely free! So the first step is to seek God, and through prayer and supplication we must ask for His divine guidance.

Keep in mind that our work does not end with prayer; it only begins there. With God's guidance and wisdom, we will be better prepared for the hard work that lies ahead: uncovering and dealing with the root causes that instigated the family breakdown.

A Step-by-Step Approach

As an engineer by education and training, my mind has been conditioned to deal with problems in a systematic and logical fashion. Dealing with problems in a linear, step-by-step way usually leads to a better solution. The same is true when trying to fix a broken relationship. If you take a careful and thoughtful approach, you will discover that the answers to your difficulties are not as elusive as you once believed. Let's go through a step-by-step method for healing your relationships:

1. List the issues from your perspective. Take the time to write them down in complete sentences, trying to illustrate with words what you think the problems are. Make each point a stand-alone sentence – a statement that can be understood on its own. It should be a complete thought.

2. List the issues from your loved one's perspective. Just as you listed your concerns in Step 1, now you will do it from their point of view. Try your best to put yourself in the other person's position and look at the problem the way you think they would. This step is critically important because it forces you to understand how the other person feels and why you think they feel that way. If you can do this, then you can begin to figure out how to best approach them to resolve the conflict.

3. After you have created these two lists, decide which of the items from your list are the most important and why. Be clear about the reasons why something is so important to you. Write the reasons below each of the issues. Again, use complete sentences to articulate why these particular issues are of utmost importance to you.

4. Now do the same for the other person's issues. Imagine that you are that person and pick the issues that you think they would consider most important. Next, as you did in Step 3, try to articulate in complete sentences why they might think these are the most important issues.

5. Write a list of the things that you want to be sure to say to the other person when the time comes to meet. Don't rely on your memory to see you through that tense moment – write it all down. Whatever you want to say, make sure that you articulate it in a non-threatening way and in the spirit of being helpful, not hurtful. State things in a personal way. Statements such as "I feel that what you said was wrong because…" or "I was disappointed and hurt by what you said to me because…" or "I know that you feel that what I did was wrong because…" are a good way to state a point without being accusatory.

6. Once you have exhausted the issues and reasons for both your side and theirs, plan a meeting with them. Carefully consider the time and place for this meeting. Pick a time that leaves plenty of room for long discussions. Pick a place that gives you both plenty of privacy and no interruptions.

7. At the meeting, start by setting the right tone. Here are a few things that you must do:

    a. Say that you want nothing more than for you both to resolve the argument and resume a loving and productive relationship.
    b. Say how sorry you are that the two of you have had this fight and how you are certain that it can be resolved.

    c. Tell them that you love them and even though you were angry with them before, you are no longer angry with them now. Also say that you realize that they were angry with you. You may even recognize that they may still be angry with you, but that you hope the two of you can move beyond the anger and restore your loving relationship.

    d. If you were hurt in the fight, tell them so. But say it in a way that merely expresses your disappointment about being hurt, not in a way that accuses them. If you recognize that they feel you hurt them, too, then say, "I realize that you felt hurt by what I said or did. I'm sorry for that. I hope that once we've talked about it, we can forgive and forget."

    e. Let them know that you want to hear them out, but that there must be rules about how the discussion will proceed so that everything remains civil. Agree to listen to each other. Agree not to interrupt each other, or raise your voices. Most importantly, agree that the past will only be discussed to help the relationship move forward, and not to point fingers. Remember that rehashing the past is of no use!

8. Once the conversation starts, make sure that you remain focused on the issues. Try to speak about only one issue at a time. This is why it was so important to prepare your list before hand. It is of paramount importance that an issue is fully discussed without jumping from one point to the next. Seek resolution to the issue. Try to discuss it until both of you are satisfied that it has been covered. Make an agreement on the issue if you can, and state what each person will do from then on to avoid future problems. Repeat this until all issues have been discussed and agreed upon. This can take a long time! Don't rush through it. Don't minimize how important it is! Do this right and you will increase your chances of not having a repeat performance later in life.

9. Once the issues have been discussed, the next important step is to define what you each want from your New and Improved Relationship. What do you want it to be like? Since we cannot change the past, we must focus on where we are going from

here. So work on agreements that move the relationship forward. Some of the most important agreements to make are:

a. The past will not be rehashed.
b. Each of you will try to forget the past events that led to the fight.
c. Each of you promises not to use past events as weapons in future conversations.
d. Each of you promises to listen more intently to each other and not to repeat the behaviors that led to the fight in the first place.
e. You will do your very best to keep the lines of communication open, and not to wait until something explodes inside either person before you talk about whatever is bothering you.

Now for the hard part! I know you probably thought that Steps 1 through 9 were the most difficult parts – no doubt they were tough. But *the hardest part is keeping the promises you made in Step 9.* Maintaining a healthy relationship is where the most challenging work comes in! Commit to each other that you will apply your best and most honest efforts toward keeping a loving and productive relationship between you.

Maintaining healthy relationships is not easy. It takes hard work. But the fruits of our labor are wonderful, happy, productive, and loving relationships. These are the kinds of relationships that God wants us to have. These are the kinds of relationships we all want to have!

CHAPTER SIX

Preparing for Reconciliation

I believe that the most powerful weapon in any Christian's arsenal is prayer. I also believe that it is the most underutilized! I confess that I do not spend nearly as much time as I should in prayer. If we spent more time in earnest prayer seeking God's will and guidance, we would solve all of the world's problems. World hunger would be no match for our prayers. Cancer would be a thing of the past. The number of heart attacks and stress-related illnesses would be near zero. Poverty would be extinct. Murders would shock us rather than be a normal part of the evening news. Racism would be part of our history books, but not part of our daily lives. Churches – not prisons – would be filled to capacity. If we prayed more, kids in high schools would be shooting baskets rather than bullets. The power of prayer is completely untapped. Thus, the very first step in preparing for reconciliation is to pray!

Pray for wisdom and patience

Matthew 17:19-21

Then the disciples came to Jesus in private and asked, "Why couldn't we drive it out?" He replied, "Because you have so little faith. I tell you the truth, if you have faith as small as a mustard seed, you can say to this mountain, 'Move from here to there' and it will move. Nothing will be impossible for you."

Have you ever seen a mustard seed? It's as tiny as the head of a pin. Yet Jesus made it clear that if our faith was only that big we could move mountains with our prayers. In His name we could command a mountain to move, and it would! The power we have through prayer is awesome. Furthermore, the Lord promises He will deliver what we earnestly and faithfully pray for.

Mark 11:24-25

Therefore I tell you, whatever you ask for in prayer, believe that you have received it, and it will be yours. And when you stand in prayer, if you hold anything against anyone, forgive him, so that your Father in heaven may forgive you your sins.

God tells us to ask Him and it shall be given. Pray and He will answer. He does not promise to answer the way we would want Him to. We must believe that He knows better than we what we need and when we need it. Trust God and His perfect will. Pray that His will be done.

If your relationship with someone you love is broken, you need to pray! You need to ask God for wisdom like Solomon did:

1 Kings 3:9-10

"So give your servant a discerning heart to govern your people and to distinguish between right and wrong. For who is able to govern this great people of yours?" The Lord was pleased that Solomon had asked for this.

God was pleased with Solomon! He could have asked for anything and God would have honored his prayer. Yet Solomon asked for wisdom. Who among us could not use a healthy dose of wisdom? You need wisdom if you are going to deal effectively with a broken relationship. You also need patience. Pray for it.

Forgive...even before they ask for forgiveness

Matthew 6:9-14

"This, then, is how you should pray: Our Father in heaven,

hollowed be your name, your kingdom come, your will be done on earth as it is in heaven. Give us today our daily bread. Forgive our debts, as we also have forgiven our debtors. And lead us not into temptation, but deliver us from the evil one. For, if you forgive men when they sin against you, your heavenly Father will also forgive you. But if you do not forgive men their sins, your Father in heaven will not forgive your sins."

Jesus taught us how to pray. This simple yet profoundly powerful prayer is more elegant and beautiful than any I have ever heard. Forgiveness is so important to God that it was included as a main part of this very short prayer. The Lord's Prayer includes only a handful of basic concepts. First, we are told to praise God's name – *hollowed be your name*. Second, we are taught to ask for what we need – *give us today our daily bread*. Next, we are commanded to ask for and grant forgiveness. Finally, we must ask for deliverance from evil. That's it. Of all the things Jesus could have chosen to include in this greatest of all prayers, He chose forgiveness as a key element.

I grew up in the Catholic Church. I attended a Catholic high school. Reciting the Our Father was a daily routine. But if you take careful note of this prayer you find it to be a bit different than the one many of us were taught to recite. Most of us learned to recite it saying "forgive us our trespasses as we forgive those who trespass against us" or "forgive us our debts as we forgive our debtors." There is one small yet crucial detail that is lost in that translation. In the King James Version of the New Testament, Jesus' words are "forgive us our debts as *we also have forgiven* our debtors." This version of Jesus' prayer clearly implies that we must have already forgiven those who sinned against us before we can ask for forgiveness! It does not say that we must wait for the person to ask for forgiveness before we grant it. It says to forgive them before we ask for forgiveness for our own sins.

Forgiving someone who has sinned against us has a healing effect on us. It allows us to let go of our anger and bitterness, and it frees us to think clearly. It helps calm our spirit and puts us at peace. Forgiving someone is as much for our good – perhaps even more so – as it is for the benefit of the person we are forgiving.

Pray for the people with whom you are feuding

<u>Matthew 5:43-45</u>

You have heard that it was said, "Love your neighbor and hate your enemy." But I tell you: Love your enemies and pray for those who persecute you, that you may be sons of your Father in heaven.

Jesus wants us to pray for our enemies! How much more, then, are we to pray for those we love – for our families and friends? Once again Scripture is clear. It doesn't say "pray for those you get along with," or "wait until you are no longer feuding with someone to pray for them." It tells us to pray for those who would persecute us. We can take comfort in the fact that Jesus does not ask us to do something that He was not willing to do Himself:

<u>Luke 23:33-34</u>

When they came to the place called the Skull, there they crucified him, along with the criminals – one on his right, the other on his left. Jesus said, "Father, forgive them, for they do not know what they are doing."

Jesus prayed that God would have mercy on His enemies. He interceded for them. How could He have done that if He had not already forgiven them in His human heart first? There He was, hanging by nails, only moments away from His death and He's asking for God to forgive the very men that drove the nails through His hands and feet. Yet we struggle to pray for and forgive someone who said the wrong thing, or who took something from us?

Be prepared to listen to the other person

<u>Proverbs 1:5</u>

Let the wise listen and add to their learning...

Listening is an active sport. We must prepare ourselves to listen. We must train ourselves to listen. Sadly, most of us have a natural inclination toward being heard rather than hearing someone else. Rather than processing what we are hearing, we tune it out and focus instead on developing what we want to say next.

When we listen to people, they feel important. They feel respected, valued and acknowledged. Poor listening is a debilitating weakness that minimizes our ability to have effective communications and reduces our ability to influence others.

Listening must be practiced. It is a skill that takes time to learn. Some of the basic principles of good listening are:

- Don't create or tolerate distractions
- Give positive, nonverbal feedback as you are listening
- Ask only important clarification questions
- Avoid going off on a tangent
- Be patient
- Visualize as you listen
- Avoid giving too much thought to what you want to say next. Listen first, then if necessary, pause to formulate a question or a response

If we learn to listen better, we will have better relationships. Listening is not just half of communication; it's most of it!

One final note on listening:

James 1:19-20

> *My dear brothers, take note of this: Everyone should be quick to listen, slow to speak and slow to become angry, for man's anger does not bring about the righteous life that God desires.*

Listen with patience. Speak only after you have carefully considered what you just heard. Think before you speak. It does not take that long. Sometimes, just pausing for a moment before speaking can be enough to help us formulate ideas and say things more clearly. You've never heard someone say, "Wow, I'm really sorry I took the time to think before I spoke." Instead, we usually hear, "I sure wish I had thought about that before I opened my big mouth!" Listen, think, and then speak – in that order!

What do you want the relationship to be like?

Do you make to-do lists? Do you write down objectives for business or personal goals? Why do we write things down? One reason is because we simply cannot remember everything. If you always try to rely on your memory, you are guaranteed only one thing: you will forget something! It is important to write down your wishes for your relationship with a family member. Doing so will help you think about how you want to treat that person and how you would like him or her to treat you. It will help you internalize and visualize the positives in your relationship, and will help you identify the "watch outs."

What are "watch outs?" They are the hot button issues in your relationship – the things that will inevitably lead to a negative reaction if they come up. Perhaps it's some of the things you say, or the way you may say them. Maybe it's the way you talk about your sister's job or her hobbies. Could it be the way you talk about your career, your friends or your house? Maybe you flaunt your wealth and you know it really irritates your brother. How about the words they sometimes use when speaking about your career choice, the college your kids attend, or the neighborhood you live in. Perhaps they make fun of your Christian beliefs. Whatever it is, if we are going to have a healthy relationship with someone, we must pay attention at his or her preferences and opinions. We must understand what turns them on and what turns them off. We must help them understand the same about us. So write it down. Talk about it. Pray about it. Do something about it!

Convince yourself not be angry or defensive

<u>Proverbs 15:1-2</u>

A gentle answer turns away wrath, but a harsh word stirs up anger. The tongue of the wise commends knowledge, but the mouth of the fool gushes folly.

Managing our Words and Attitudes

Our words and the attitude with which we express them make our demeanor quite clear. If we choose angry words and say them with fire in our eyes, the message we send and its intent will be clearly understood. Moreover, our angry words and gruff attitude will be reciprocated with equally harsh words and attitudes from those we attack. On the other hand, if we choose to answer with patience, kindness, and love, we deflect any anger and wrath the other person may be feeling. Our choice of words and the way in which we say them is absolutely critical to maintaining healthy relationships and to healing those that are broken.

Put in another way:

Our Words + Our Attitude = Our Message

Our Message + Their Attitude = Their Response

And since their attitude is a direct function of our message, then:

Their Response = A Reflection of our Words and Attitude

Is it any surprise that we get back something that looks remarkably similar to what we dish out? If you send out angry words, angry words will come back to you, magnified. It's as simple as the Law of the Harvest.

Years ago the senior pastor at the church I attend preached a powerful sermon on the Law of the Harvest. The principles of the law he outlined are very basic, yet fundamentally profound. They are:

Law #1

It is impossible to reap until you have sown

Law #2

It is impossible to reap something other than what you have sown

Law #3

You not only reap what you sow, you get more of it!

Law #4

It is impossible to reap if you quit

These powerful principles explain how we create our own realities. If we sow anger and hate, that's what we will reap. Nothing else can come of it! That would be like expecting to get tomatoes after planting corn seeds. If you plant tomatoes, you get tomatoes. Period. No other possible outcome should be expected. So plant love if you want to get love back. Not only is the outcome predetermined by the seed we plant, but we can expect it to increase in return. If we plant anger, we'll get explosive anger back. If we fire off hateful words, we should expect cannonball-sized hateful words to come flying back at us. That's the third law of the harvest: you not only reap what you sow, but you get lots of it back! So choose what you plant wisely. Finally, if you don't even try to plant a seed, you can forget about getting any harvest.

You want kind words spoken towards you? Start speaking kind words. It will spread. You want to feel loved? Start loving. It will spread. You want people to pray for you? Start praying for them. It will spread. You want to have trust in your relationships? Start trusting. It will spread. You want honest communications? Start communicating honestly. It will spread.

And the list goes on and on. Whatever behavior you want to see in your family relationships, plant the right seed for it and you will reap what you planted many times over. Just remember that the opposite is most certainly true as well!

Think Positive

If you do a quick search on the titles of self-help books you will find thousands of books and articles on the subject of positive thinking, self-talk and self-motivation. These are not new concepts. People have been talking themselves into things since the beginning of time. Somehow we can summon the courage to jump out of an airplane with nothing but some nylon strapped to our back, or climb a steep mountain with a rope tied about our waist, tempting death at every turn. When was the last time you heard of an Olympic athlete telling herself, "I'm not going to win, I'm not going to win, I'm not going to win?" If she did, she surely would not win. Instead, gold medal winners convince themselves that they are going to run the best race of their lives every time. They tell themselves over and over that they will win.

Motivational speakers are fond of telling their audiences to believe in themselves, set goals for themselves, and start acting in ways that are consistent with those goals. They say that one should visualize the goal as having already been achieved; thereby creating a positive energy within themselves that motivates them to move in the direction of the goal. Who could argue with that logic? We teach our children about how the Little Engine That Could strained to the top of a mighty hill chugging the familiar mantra "I think I can, I think I can, I think I can." What if the message was "Maybe I can't, maybe I can't, maybe I can't"? Would the little engine make it over the top? Probably not.

Think yourself into a positive attitude. Think yourself into being calm, focused and peaceful. Tell yourself over and over that you are not going to be defensive and that you will not attack your family member. Repeat it over and over again in your head. Say it out loud. Make it your new reality. Sounds silly? I bet it's not half as silly as some of the things that you and your estranged family member argued about in the first place.

Remember the good traits in the person you are fighting with and why you care about them

We live in a society that thrives on the negative. You have only to watch the evening television news to see a clear pattern. Usually, the news that is reported first is the worst news of the day. We hear about all the murders, fires, accidents, battles, bombings and other terrorist attacks. We hear reports of anti-Semitic bigots attacking Jewish temples. We hear about the brutal rape of a young woman who was attacked while jogging in the park. We are not shocked anymore when we hear the report of a woman who killed five of her children by drowning them, or how a teenager entered his high school, opened fire with semi-automatic weapons and killed a dozen of his classmates. We watch programs that show people getting arrested by the police and we stay frozen to the television screen as we watch the replays of high speed police chases that end in tragedy. Our society feeds on the negative!

Is it any surprise that we would also focus on the negative rather than the positive aspects of a relationship? Even in our closest relationships we dwell on the negative aspects, thinking more often about what we don't like rather than the positive traits that caused us to love the person in the first place. We usually treat the people closest to us with the least amount of respect. We take each other for granted. We have no problem paying a compliment to someone at work, but we struggle to say something nice to our brother or sister at home.

If you are in an estranged and broken relationship with someone you love, take the time to consider what is good about him or her. Give serious thought and high priority to what you like and love about that person. Remember with fondness the happy times you spent together. When we pay more attention to the positive traits in someone, they become easier to love. When we let the positive traits overshadow the negative ones, suddenly the person appears completely different – and much more attractive – in our eyes and in our heart.

A note of caution: if we seek and expect perfection in our family members, we will be sorely disappointed. Only God is perfect. What's more, if we try to compare our loved one to others, we set ourselves up for a letdown. We've all heard the saying that *the grass is always greener on the other side of the fence*. This refers to our tendency to look at our neighbor with envy and wish that we had what he has. We look at his home and wish we could have one just as spacious. We think that his job is better than ours. We see his relationships with his relatives and we wish that ours could be as good. Well, as was previously stated, if the grass appears greener on the other side of the fence, it may be because it's being fertilized. It may be because your neighbor is taking really good care of that grass. Maybe he's pulling weeds, keeping the hedges nicely trimmed, raking up the dead leaves, and picking up the fallen tree branches before he goes to work every morning. In other words, he's tending his yard carefully, and working on it diligently!

Similarly, if we work on our relationships, if we fertilize them with kind words and positive thoughts, we will have better relationships. If we fuss over our relationships by getting rid of the weeds – those negative things that we don't like – we will have better relationships. If we keep our relationships free of debris by talking about things that bother us before they pile up like fallen leaves that smother the grass beneath them, then we will have better relationships. *If we work hard at it, we will have better relationships.*

In his Epistle to the Romans, Paul provides very clear direction on how we are to deal with relationships:

Romans 12:9–21

⁹Love must be sincere. Hate what is evil; cling to what is good. ¹⁰Be devoted to one another in brotherly love. Honor one another above yourselves. ¹¹Never be lacking in zeal, but keep your spiritual fervor, serving the Lord. ¹²Be joyful *in hope, patient in affliction, faithful in prayer. ¹³Share with God's people who are in need. Practice hospitality.*

¹⁴Bless those who persecute you; bless and do not curse. ¹⁵Rejoice with those who rejoice; mourn with those who mourn. ¹⁶Live in harmony with one another. Do not be proud, but be willing to associate with people of low position. Do not be conceited.

¹⁷Do not repay anyone evil for evil. Be careful to do what is right in the eyes of everybody. ¹⁸If it is possible, as far as it depends on you, live at peace with everyone. ¹⁹Do not take revenge, my friends, but leave room for God's wrath, for it is written: "It is mine to avenge; I will repay," says the Lord. ²⁰On the contrary: "If your enemy is hungry, feed him; if he is thirsty, give him something to drink. In doing this, you will heap burning coals on his head." ²¹Do not be overcome by evil, but overcome evil with good.

In this passage Paul explains the essence of love; the love that we must have between family members. It is a love that is sincere and without pretense. Paul is referring to love that is more than emotion; he is calling us to action. He also provides clear direction on a few other points:

1. He exhorts us to be strong in our zeal, referring to our spiritual desire. If our spiritual connection with God remains strong, then we will have a divine ability to deal with the world around us.

2. Paul reminds us to keep our joy. Being happy and positive is a personal choice. We must choose joy. If we commit ourselves to remaining happy, there is nothing or no one who can steal that away from us.

3. Most importantly in this passage, we are told to remain patient in our pain and faithful in our prayer.

Proverbs 19:11

A man's wisdom gives him patience; it is to his glory to overlook an offense.

Dealing with difficult relationships and people takes a healthy amount of patience. It is our wisdom that gives us our patience. So once again we come back to the need to pray for both wisdom and patience. Without wisdom and patience, healthy and productive relationships will be difficult at best.

4. Paul is also very clear about how we are to act toward someone who we feel has done us wrong.

    ···Do not take revenge, my friends, but leave room for God's wrath, for it is written: "It is mine to avenge; I will repay," says the Lord. On the contrary: "If your enemy is hungry, feed him; if he is thirsty, give him something to drink. In doing this, you will heap burning coals on his head." Do not be overcome by evil, but overcome evil with good...

We mustn't have a vengeful heart. In fact, according to God's word, quite the contrary is the case. If we respond to aggression with kindness we "heap coals of fire on his head." We win with kindness, not anger. We respond with love, not hate. We come back with prayers, not curses.

CHAPTER SEVEN

Keeping the Peace

Matthew 5:1-10

Now when he saw the crowd, he went up on a mountainside and sat down. His disciples came to him and he began to teach them, saying: 'Blessed are the poor in spirit, for theirs is the kingdom of heaven. Blessed are those who mourn, for they will be comforted. Blessed are the meek, for they will inherit the earth. Blessed are those who hunger and thirst for righteousness, for they will be filled. Blessed are the merciful, for they will be shown mercy. Blessed are the pure in heart, for they will see God. Blessed are the peacemakers, for they will be called the sons of God. Blessed are those who are persecuted because of righteousness, for theirs is the kingdom of heaven'."

Perhaps one of the hardest things about fixing broken relationships is keeping them from breaking again. If there is one thing that I've noticed about arguing with someone you love, it is this: after we have apologized, talked about the situation, resolved it, and made peace with each other, it does not take long to become complacent about the relationship again. When that happens we fall back into the same old habits that may have caused the broken relationship in the first place. Keeping relationships whole requires hard work. Maintaining the peace requires us to be on alert for things that may get in the way of keeping that peace.

When Jesus gave his disciples the beatitudes, He gave us a road map for how we should behave. In one of the beatitudes He exhorts us to be peacekeepers and He promises that only then will we be called the son's (and daughters!) of God.

Psalm 34:14

Turn from evil and do good; seek peace and pursue it.

Psalm 29:11

The Lord gives strength to His people; the Lord blesses His people with peace.

He wants us to be peacekeepers. He *expects* us to be peacekeepers.

Mark 9:50

Salt is good, but if it loses its saltiness, how can you make it salty again? Have salt in yourselves and be at peace with each other.

This last verse is profound. Think of it. The distinctive mark of discipleship typified by salt is allegiance to Jesus Christ and the Gospel. Differences are resolved and peace is restored only when we recognize in one another a common commitment to Jesus and to the Gospel. So, be salt in a relationship and bring peace to yourself and to the one you love.

Focus on positive aspects of your relationship

You know the old adage that *there are only two things in life that are certain; death and taxes – and you don't have to pay your taxes!* Well, we can add one more to that list of certain things: *in every relationship there will be some things you like and some things you don't.* If you wait until you find perfection to develop relationships with people, you will be lonely for a very long time.

Consider your workplace for a moment; no doubt you can think of things you like and things you don't like about it. How about your church? No doubt there are some things you like about it, and some you don't. Think of your best friend. Surely, there are one or two things that you wish you could change about him or her. Nothing in life is perfect.

However, while we have no choice but to settle for less than perfection in people, places, and relationships, we do have a choice about where we place our focus. In our workplace we can focus on the good things about our work; the benefits, flexible hours, vacation time, some fun co-workers, and good health benefits. Or we can let having a difficult boss or co-worker get us down and leave us feeling and acting negative. In our church we can complain about the nursery care for children or about the choir singing off key, or we can be grateful for a gifted pastor and teacher. We can focus on our best friend's shortcomings, or we can choose to highlight her good traits. We can find reasons to criticize people, or we can build them up with words of encouragement. But we have to decide – we can't do both. Focusing on the negative aspects of a relationship, place, or person robs us of the ability to fully appreciate the joy of what is good about them. We have a choice. Choose the positive!

Live the relationship in the present and future

There are two things we should do with the past: remember it fondly and learn from it. There are two things we should not do with the past: dwell on it and try to relive it. Wise people learn from their past experiences and figure out a way to apply what they have learned to create a better present and the possibility of a brighter future. This is incredibly important in dealing with our relationships.

Throughout this book we have examined why relationships break down, when they break down, the common themes among broken relationships, how to create an environment in which healing can begin, and how to go about fixing a broken relationship. In essence, we have examined how to use what we have learned from the past to change our present and create the possibility of a better future. That's what our goal must be. That is why we go through the agony of dealing with broken relationships. We study the past to help us make better decisions in the present. We don't dwell on it, for doing so would prevent us from making strives forward. If we get hung up on the past, we will never experience the liberating power of fixing today's problem so we can be happy tomorrow. When we hang on to the past, we miss the world as it goes marching by, right before our eyes. What a shame to live in the past and miss the glorious present!

Let us strive to make the most of today, for we can do nothing about changing yesterday, and we don't know what tomorrow holds. Answer this question: What would you want to have your relationship with your loved one to be like if today was the last day or your life? Whatever your answer, make that your reality today! It's entirely up to you.

Romans 12:18

If it is possible, as far as it depends on you, live at peace with everyone.

Keep open channels of communication

One thing is certain: if we are going to keep the peace in a relationship, it must be grounded in trust. Trust is achieved through open, honest, complete and compassionate communication. Arguably, the most important of these communication characteristics is that it be compassionate. Compassionate communications implies that we keep the other person's needs in mind when we are speaking with them. We ground our communications in love and concern for our family member, and we do our best to speak from a kind and gentle heart rather than a hardened, argumentative spirit.

Examine your heart, your spirit and your mind. Make sure that they are in the right place. Make sure that you are not being hurtful or spiteful with your words just because you feel that the other person treated you poorly. Practice the principles we've discussed in this text, and be a model for others to emulate when it comes to healthy, loving communication among family members.

Have a servant spirit

Mark 9:33-35

They came to Capernaum. When He was in the house, He asked them, "What were you arguing about on the road?" But they kept quiet because on the way they had argued about who was the greatest. Sitting down, Jesus called the Twelve and said, "If anyone wants to be first, he must be the very last, and the servant of all."

<u>John 13:4-5</u>

...so He got up from the meal, took off his outer clothing, and wrapped a towel around His waist. After that, He poured water into a basin and began to wash His disciple's feet, drying them with the towel that was wrapped around Him."

In performing the humbling task of washing His disciple's feet – something usually reserved for the lowest servants in a household – Jesus was making a powerful statement about servanthood. He even waited until after the meal had already begun, rather than washing their feet when they first arrived. No one else had volunteered to do the dirty work. In fact, you can probably imagine a few of the disciples grumbling because there was no servant available to wash their feet before dinner. Jesus waited until after the dinner had started to emphasize His point. It was a lesson in humility, but it also set forth the example of selfless service that He would soon exemplify again on the cross.

Just as Jesus did for His disciples, we must also do for our families. We must have a servant attitude and enough humility to do whatever needs to be done. That especially includes doing what needs to be done to care for and nurture our family relationships.

Love unconditionally

<u>1 Corinthians 13:4-13</u>

Love is patient, love is kind. It does not envy, it does not boast, it is not proud. It is not rude, it is not self-seeking, it is not easily angered, it keeps no records of wrongs. Love does not delight in evil, but rejoices with the truth. It always protects, always trusts, always hopes, always perseveres. Love never fails. But where there are prophecies they will cease; where there are tongues, they will be stilled; where there is knowledge, it will pass away. For we know in part and we prophesy in part, but when perfection comes, the imperfect disappears. When I was a child, I talked like a child, I reasoned like a child. When I became a man, I put childish ways behind me. Now we see but a poor reflection as in a mirror, then we shall see face to face. Now I know in part, then I shall know fully, even as I am fully known. And now these three remain: faith, hope and love. But the greatest of these is love.

Have you been patient with the family member you are fighting with? Have you been kind to them? Think back on your behavior with them. Have you been rude? Are you keeping track of the things they do to irritate you so that you can bring them up later? Are you speaking the truth to them? Or are you acting like a child – holding a grudge and refusing to play nice with them as if you were a third grader? This is where the rubber meets the road. It's time you take a hard look at your own behaviors. It's time for you to be honest with yourself. Lock yourself up in a closet somewhere and have a serious talk with yourself. Be honest with yourself. After all, it would be supremely stupid to lie to yourself. Answer these questions:

Do you still love the person you are fighting with?

Have you asked them for forgiveness? Have you forgiven them?

Whatever the argument was about, is it really worth ending the relationship?

Is your pride getting in the way of reconciliation?

Why can't you simply forget what was done or said?

How would you feel if you got a phone call this moment letting you know that your family member had suddenly died?

Are you letting your anger cloud your judgment?

Are you waiting for them to start the reconciliation process?

Can you look your children in the eyes and explain why they can't see Uncle George or Aunt Betsy? Can you, with a clear conscience, explain that they will not be able to see their cousins anymore? Will you be able to rationalize to them why they cannot spend any more summers with Grandma or Grandpa?

How long will you be stubborn?

Now that you have read this book and asked yourself the questions listed above, do you still feel justified in your anger and remain committed to not fixing your relationship? If you can remain steadfast in your selfish attitude and disregard the needs of those around you; if you are not concerned with the legacy you leave behind; if you are confident that God will understand your reasons for perpetuating a rift within one of his most sacred creations – the family; if you just don't care about all that, then there is only one thing left to say:

See you at the wake.

ABOUT THE AUTHOR

Anthony López is the author of *The Legacy Leader: Leadership With A Purpose, Breakthrough Thinking: The Legacy Leader's Role In Driving Innovation, The Leader's Lobotomy: The Legacy Leader Avoids Promotion Induced Amnesia, The Legacy Leader: 2nd Edition, and The Leader In the Mirror: The Legacy Leader's Critical Self-Assessment.* He is also the author of two Christian books titled: *See You At The Wake: Healing Relationships Before It's Too Late* and *Jag: Christian Lessons From My Golden Retriever.* He is a popular motivational speaker, and is a recognized expert on leadership and management. Tony began his career as a US Air Force officer where he served as a flight test director and program manager. Tony later served as a human resources officer in the Air Force Reserves. He joined Johnson & Johnson in 1991 and held leadership positions in corporate engineering, manufacturing, marketing, communications, and general management. Later he was global vice president for marketing at ConMed. Most recently Tony was the Senior Vice President and General Manger for CareFusion Respiratory Systems. Tony is also president of L&L Associates, a leadership and management consulting group he founded in 2000. He was an adjunct professor at the Richard T. Dormer School of Business and Management Sciences at Indiana Purdue University. Tony holds a BS in electrical engineering, an MS in engineering management, and is a graduate of the Department of Defense Equal Opportunity Management Institute. You can contact Tony at: ablopez85@yahoo.com. For more information, please visit www.thelegacyleader.net.